LIFE WITHIN
HIDDEN WORLDS

Other titles in the
Forensic Psychotherapy Monograph Series

Forensic Psychotherapy and Psychopathology: Winnicottian Perspectives, edited by Brett Kahr

Violence: A Public Health Menace and a Public Health Approach, edited by Sandra L. Bloom

LIFE WITHIN HIDDEN WORLDS
Psychotherapy in Prisons

Edited by

Jessica Williams Saunders

Foreword by

Sir David Ramsbotham

Forensic Psychotherapy Monograph Series

Series Editor
Brett Kahr

Honorary Consultant
Estela Welldon

London & New York
KARNAC BOOKS

In memory of the late Dr Murray Cox,
whose thoughts and reflections
have inspired and illuminated my path
in these hidden worlds

First published in 2001 by
H. Karnac (Books) Ltd.
6 Pembroke Buildings, Scrubs Lane, London NW10 6RE
A subsidiary of Other Press LLC, New York

British Library Cataloguing in Publication Data

A C.I.P for this book is available from the British Library

ISBN: 1 85575 219 0

10 9 8 7 6 5 4 3 2 1

Edited, designed, and produced by Communication Crafts
Printed in Great Britain by Polestar Wheatons Ltd, Exeter

www.karnacbooks.com

CONTENTS

v

SERIES FOREWORD

Brett Kahr

School of Psychotherapy and Counselling,
Regent's College, London

Throughout most of human history, our ancestors have done rather poorly when dealing with acts of violence. To cite but one of many shocking examples, let us perhaps recall a case from 1801, of an English boy aged only 13, who was executed by hanging on the gallows at Tyburn. What was his crime? It seems that he had been condemned to die for having stolen a spoon (Westwick, 1940).

In most cases, our predecessors have either *ignored* murderousness and aggression, as in the case of Graeco–Roman infanticide, which occurred so regularly in the ancient world that it acquired an almost normative status (deMause, 1974; Kahr, 1994); or they have *punished* murderousness and destruction with retaliatory sadism, a form of unconscious identification with the aggressor. Any history of criminology will readily reveal the cruel punishments inflicted upon prisoners throughout the ages, ranging from beatings and stockades, to more severe forms of torture, culminating in eviscerations, beheadings, or lynchings.

Only during the last one hundred years have we begun to develop the capacity to respond more intelligently and more humanely to acts of dangerousness and destruction. Since the advent of psychoanalysis, we now have access to a much deeper understanding both of the aetiology of aggressive acts and of their treatment; and nowadays we need no longer ignore criminals or abuse them—instead, we can provide compassion and containment, as well as conduct research that can help to prevent future acts of violence.

The modern discipline of forensic psychotherapy, which can be defined, quite simply, as the use of psychoanalytically orientated "talking therapy" to treat violent, offender patients, stems directly from the work of Sigmund Freud. Almost one hundred years ago, at a meeting of the Vienna Psycho-Analytical Society, held on 6 February 1907, Sigmund Freud anticipated the clarion call of contemporary forensic psychotherapists when he bemoaned the often horrible treatment of mentally ill offenders, in a discussion on the psychology of vagrancy. According to Otto Rank, Freud's secretary at the time, the founder of psychoanalysis expressed his sorrow at the "nonsensical treatment of these people in prisons" (quoted in Nunberg & Federn, 1962, p. 108).

Many of the early psychoanalysts preoccupied themselves with forensic topics. Hanns Sachs, himself a trained lawyer, and Marie Bonaparte, the French princess who wrote about the cruelty of war, spoke fiercely against capital punishment. Sachs, one of the first members of Freud's secret committee, regarded the death penalty for offenders as an example of group sadism (Moellenhoff, 1966). Bonaparte, who had studied various murderers throughout her career, had actually lobbied politicians in America to free the convicted killer Caryl Chessman, during his sentence on Death Row at the California State Prison in San Quentin, albeit unsuccessfully (Bertin, 1982).

Some years later, Melanie Klein concluded her first book, the landmark text *Die Psychoanalyse des Kindes* [*The Psycho-Analysis of Children*], with resounding passion about the problem of violence. Mrs Klein noted that acts of criminality invariably stem from disturbances in childhood, and that if young people could receive access to psychoanalytic treatment at any early age, then much cruelty could be prevented in later years. Klein expressed the hope that: "If every child who shows disturbances that are at all severe were to be analysed in good time, a great number of these people who later end up in prisons or lunatic asylums, or who go completely to pieces, would be saved from such a fate and be able to develop a normal life" (1932, p. 374).

Shortly after the publication of Klein's transformative book, Atwell Westwick, a Judge of the Superior Court of Santa Barbara,

California, published a little-known though highly inspiring article, "Criminology and Psychoanalysis" (1940), in the *Psychoanalytic Quarterly*. Westwick may well be the first judge to commit himself in print to the value of psychoanalysis in the study of criminality, arguing that punishment of the forensic patient remains, in fact, a sheer waste of time. With foresight, Judge Westwick queried, "Can we not, in our well nigh hopeless and overwhelming struggle with the problems of delinquency and crime, profit by medical experience with the problems of health and disease? Will we not, eventually, terminate the senseless policy of sitting idly by until misbehavior occurs, often with irreparable damage, then dumping the delinquent into the juvenile court or reformatory and dumping the criminal into prison?" (p. 281). Westwick noted that we should, instead, train judges, probation officers, social workers, as well as teachers and parents, in the precepts of psychoanalysis, in order to arrive at a more sensitive, non-punitive understanding of the nature of criminality. He opined: "When we shall have succeeded in committing society to such a program, when we see it launched definitely upon the venture, as in time it surely will be—then shall we have erected an appropriate memorial to Sigmund Freud" (p. 281).

In more recent years, the field of forensic psychotherapy has become increasingly well constellated. Building upon the pioneering contributions of such psychoanalysts and psychotherapists as Edward Glover, Grace Pailthorpe, Melitta Schmideberg, and more recently Murray Cox, Ismond Rosen, Estela Welldon, and others too numerous to mention, forensic psychotherapy has now become an increasingly formalized discipline that can be dated to the inauguration of the International Association for Forensic Psychotherapy and to the first annual conference, held at St. Bartholomew's Hospital in London in 1991. The profession now boasts a more robust foundation, with training courses developing in the United Kingdom and beyond. Since the inauguration of the Diploma in Forensic Psychotherapy (and subsequently the Diploma in Forensic Psychotherapeutic Studies), under the auspices of the British Postgraduate Medical Federation of the University of London in association with the Portman Clinic, students can now seek further instruction in the psychodynamic treatment of patients who act out in a dangerous and illegal manner.

The volumes in this series of books will aim to provide both practical advice and theoretical stimulation for introductory students and for senior practitioners alike. In the Karnac Books Forensic Psychotherapy Monograph Series, we will endeavour to produce a regular stream of high-quality titles, written by leading members of the profession, who will share their expertise in a concise and practice-orientated fashion. We trust that such a collection of books will help to consolidate the knowledge and experience that we have already acquired and will also provide new directions for the upcoming decades of the new century. In this way, we shall hope to plant the seeds for a more rigorous, sturdy, and wide-reaching profession of forensic psychotherapy.

As the new millennium begins to unfold, we now have an opportunity for psychotherapeutically orientated forensic mental health professionals to work in close conjunction with child psychologists and with infant mental health specialists so that the problems of violence can be tackled both preventatively and retrospectively. With the growth of the field of forensic psychotherapy, we at last have reason to be hopeful that serious criminality can be forestalled and perhaps, one day, even eradicated.

References

Bertin, C. (1982). *La Dernière Bonaparte*. Paris: Librairie Académique Perrin.

deMause, L. (1974). The evolution of childhood. In: Lloyd deMause (Ed.), *The History of Childhood* (pp. 1–73). New York: Psychohistory Press.

Kahr, B. (1994). The historical foundations of ritual abuse: an excavation of ancient infanticide. In: Valerie Sinason (Ed.), *Treating Survivors of Satanist Abuse* (pp. 45–56). London: Routledge.

Klein, M. (1932). *The Psycho-Analysis of Children*, trans. Alix Strachey. London: Hogarth Press and The Institute of Psycho-Analysis. [First published as *Die Psychoanalyse des Kindes*. Vienna: Internationaler Psychoanalytischer Verlag.]

Moellenhoff, F. (1966). Hanns Sachs, 1881–1947: the creative unconscious. In: F. Alexander, S. Eisenstein, & M. Grotjahn (Eds.), *Psychoanalytic Pioneers* (pp. 180–199). New York: Basic Books.

Nunberg, H., & Federn, E. (Eds.) (1962). *Minutes of the Vienna Psychoanalytic Society. Volume I: 1906–1908*, trans. Margarethe Nunberg. New York: International Universities Press.

Westwick, A. (1940). Criminology and Psychoanalysis. *Psychoanalytic Quarterly*, 9: 269–282.

EDITOR AND CONTRIBUTORS

Ronald Doctor, MMBBCh., MMed.Psych., MRCPsych., is Consultant Psychiatrist in Psychotherapy and College Tutor at the West Middlesex University Hospital and Ashford Hospital, Hounslow and Spelthorne CMH NHS Trust. He is Visiting Psychiatrist at the Max Glatt Unit, Wormwood Scrubs Prison, and a supervisor on the Forensic Psychotherapy Course at the Tavistock and Portman NHS Trust. He is an Associate Member of the British Psychoanalytical Society.

Paola Franciosi, MD, MRCPsych., is a Consultant Psychotherapist at the Abraham Cowley Unit, Chertsey, Surrey, and a Visiting Consultant in a prison.

Lynn Greenwood undertook a three-year training in counselling and psychotherapy following ten years as a Management Consultant. Since then she has completed an MA in Psychotherapy and Counselling at Regent's College, London. She works as a psychotherapist at Wormwood Scrubs Prison and has a private practice. She is an English Literature graduate and has an MBA from the London Business School.

Mark Morris, BA, MBChB, MRCPsych., is Director of Therapy at Grendon Prison and a Psychiatrist in Psychotherapy. He was a former Senior Registrar at the Cassel Hospital and Consultant Psychiatrist in Psychotherapy at St Bernard's Hospital, Ealing. He is an Associate Member of the British Psychoanalytic Society.

Jessica Williams Saunders, Registered Dramatherapist, Dip. Forensic Psychotherapy, specialized in forensic work in prison and special hospital settings as a therapist and clinical supervisor over a period of nine years. She devised and performed the lead roles in two productions with her theatre company, The Theatre of Reflection, drawing inspiration for themes from her clinical practice. She has a number of publications based on her work as a clinical and theatre practitioner. She currently works as a freelance consultant.

FOREWORD

Sir David Ramsbotham

Throughout recent times, a politically controlled pendulum has swung the weight of the debate between whether security or constructive programmes to tackle re-offending should be the dominant theme in the treatment of and conditions for prisoners in our prisons. Phrases like "Prison Works" and "Prison Doesn't Work" have been bandied about as if they are absolutes, when the truth is that there can be no absolutes because there are no stereotypical prisoners or, indeed, prisons. The aim currently given to the Criminal Justice System, of which prisons are a part, is the protection of the public by the prevention of crime. In the case of prisons this could be taken as the prevention of re-crime, because sentenced prisoners would not be in prison unless they had committed, or were alleged to have committed, a crime in the first place.

For them the admirable aim "Prevent the Next Victim", adopted by Her Majesty's Young Offender Institution Lancaster Farms, would seem to apply. This requires that something positive should be done in prisons to try firstly to understand what it is that has encouraged a prisoner to offend, and secondly to do something to prevent that happening again when, as will happen to all but a handful of prisoners, they return to the community. This boils down to using the time that a prisoner is in prison to the best advantage both of the prisoner and of the community to which he or she will return. It is the very opposite of the view held by too many—including, unfortunately, officials in the Treasury—that prisons are all about containment, and that they do not need to be resourced to do more than keep people confined.

Prisoners come in all shapes and sizes and from a wide variety of backgrounds, and they present a wide spectrum of criminality. But all are individuals, with individual needs that must be assessed before it can be determined how their term of imprisonment can best be used both to their advantage and to that of the community to which they will return.

To help focus our attentions in monitoring and influencing the treatment of and conditions for prisoners—the role and responsibility of HM Inspectorate of Prisons—we have developed and adopted the concept of what we call "The Healthy Prison". This is not to enable us to league-table prisons, but to describe them in terms of the quality of the output of their treatment of prisoners. A Healthy Prison is one in which the weakest prisoners feel safe, in which all prisoners are treated with respect as fellow human beings, in which all are encouraged to improve themselves and are given the opportunity of engaging in purposeful activities to enable them to do so, and in which all are prepared for release, including being enabled to keep contact with their families. The Prison Service is now adopting this concept.

The most difficult problem that every prison system in the world faces is the care and treatment of those who commit the most outrageous crimes on their fellow men. They may well come from a background of deception, secrecy, corruption, conspiracy, and, most probably, denial of reality. These people do not lend themselves to normal custodial arrangements, based on appeal to the logic of discipline, and their care is beyond the capabilities of prison staffs. They need different treatment, which is where psychotherapists come in, not working apart from but in partnership with prison officers. Prisons are not ideal environments in which to practice psychotherapy, but they are places in which it is needed urgently. Unfortunately, too many people do not understand either the need or what the therapy can offer, and ignorance is a powerful enemy of practice.

I was therefore delighted to read that all the authors of the various chapters in this book articulated, wittingly or unwittingly, the need for Healthy Prison conditions to apply if the psychotherapeutic programmes that they either deliver or advocate are to have any chance of success. Therefore, I can relate their value to the concept, in any attempt to combat that ignorance.

In stating that there is no such thing as a stereotypical prisoner I am acknowledging that there are some who are more difficult, dangerous, and disruptive than others, who will need special treatment to prevent their reoffending. Not all prisoners will need the programme described at HMP Grendon Underwood, nor indeed that delivered either in the Max Glatt unit in HMP Wormwood Scrubs or in the special unit at HMP Holloway. All must have their needs assessed, so that what is most appropriate can be delivered. The Prison Service has the difficult task of attempting to ensure that all needs can be catered for. Its most intractable problem is with those at the extreme end of the difficult, dangerous, and disruptive spectrum, whose treatment, because of personality and other disorders, cannot solely be a matter of control. These are the prisoners whose treatment and needs are described in this book.

On the issue of safety, I am glad that mention is made of two important questions that must be asked on behalf of all those involved in such therapy. First, is prison a safe place in which to explore the inner world of prisoners who have committed some fairly horrific crimes? Second, if so, have boundaries been set up around the process to ensure that there is a chance of therapy taking place? I say that because it is important to recognize that control and therapy are not natural bedfellows in prison.

I am glad that the culture in prisons is mentioned and described—not only the culture of prisoners, but also that of prison officers. Both cultures are essentially masculine, typified by a macho bravado that is itself something of a defence mechanism both against others and for the individual. Many prison officers adopt an attitude of having to outsmart prisoners by beating them at their own game of toughness. Those officers who do not work with therapists are unaware that the prisoners for whom they are responsible can make the same emotional demands on them both. This book will help prison officers to better understand the culture of therapists—if that is the right word to use to describe their motivation and start point.

On the subject of respect, the tone is set in the Introduction, where Jessica Williams Saunders says that, despite the nature of the crimes that they have committed, she has to think of the prisoners she is treating as humans and not animals. However, her colleagues remind us of the importance of not becoming too inured to the enormity of what has happened to patients, nor of what they have done. In other words, therapists and prison officers must not lose sight of the word "humanity", enshrined in the Prison Service's own Statement of Purpose, in treating individuals as individuals and not merely cases.

Nothing is more purposeful than psychotherapy aimed at trying to help prisoners to live useful and law-abiding lives in prison and on release. It is demanding of psychotherapists, and it is demanding of prisoners. Indeed, undertaking a course requires deliberate acts of courage by both parties. Therapy is the very opposite of some of the dynamics that operate within prison walls. It is never an end in itself, but likely to be the start—or the continuation—of a process that will have to be maintained if the prisoner—or patient—is to think before acting, a process that is also required in other courses designed to correct particular manifestations of offending behaviour.

But it must be remembered that the structured environment of a prison is often a perceived safe-haven for prisoners, who find the concept of freedom frightening. It must be hoped that those who undergo therapy will feel more secure in themselves, which, in turn, can lead to a diminishing compulsion to harm others, thus making them safer candidates for release. But it is equally likely that this feeling of security in themselves is only engendered by psychotherapy, in which case it is important that arrangements are made for it to be continued in the community, if all that is gained is not to be lost.

I make these comments in the context of the Healthy Prison to illustrate my belief that psychotherapy should not be seen as antithetical to the ethos of a prison, because it is a most important tool in the constant battle to challenge the behaviour of those who represent the greatest threat to society. To ensure that this view is accepted, it is important that prison staff should understand where therapists come from, and vice versa. The value of *Life Within Hidden Worlds* is that it helps to fill that gap by explaining, simply yet graphically, the challenges that face therapists. I therefore recommend it most strongly to all those working in prisons who share the responsibility of looking after the most difficult, dangerous, and disturbed prisoners in the system. Jessica Williams Saunders is to be thanked for her initiative, and Lynn Greenwood, Ronald Doctor, Paola Franciosi, and Mark Morris are to be thanked for their contributions. I wish the book every success.

INTRODUCTION

I was sitting on a London transport bus some time ago pondering on a theme in this book that I was seeing replicated in the contributors' writing and in my own: that of offenders' capacity to seriously damage others, their own guilt for the crimes they have committed, and the responsibility they must take for their actions. This is balanced alongside concerns of a humanitarian nature about trying to understand their inner worlds and the motivation behind the crimes they commit. I glanced up and saw the following Metropolitan Police advert: "Put a Crook Away. Call Crimestoppers Anonymously. You could get a cash reward." This was accompanied by a particularly gruesome cartoon of a "thug", bearing the classic convict stubble chin and evil grimace, clinging on to the bars of his prison cell. "Oh dear", I thought to myself . . . here was I engaged in a process of putting together a book that would hopefully go some way towards opening up a dialogue about incarceration and the need for an understanding of the deeper meaning hidden in the criminal act, whilst there in front of me was an advertising slogan reflecting, no doubt, what was the majority opinion that offenders are "evil" commodities, objects that have, it would seem, a market price attached to their person.

What I hope will be apparent in this book is a view that occurs in all the writing: that people who commit crimes against another person are human, not animals, albeit with the capacity to carry out deeply disturbing, dark acts. The contributions show that if one can begin to reach beyond the criminal persona that has been erected as a defence mechanism against any kind of meaningful and intimate relationship with life, people, and experiences, then it is evident that they do have a feeling world, one that, once accessed, can be almost overwhelming in the depth of feelings encountered therein. Psychotherapy is not involved in condoning criminals' actions—only they can be accountable for these. It is, however, attempting to find a path through the dense "undergrowth" of the psychological make-up of the offender which can camouflage a true self hidden in the murky terrain that makes up the criminal's inner world.

Prisons are also murky places: places of punishment, deceptive shadow-worlds with hidden, secret dynamics and agendas. Psychotherapy is about illumination, about seeing and hearing, with a search for truth and understanding of the hidden interior landscape. Prisons are hard; psychotherapy is porous, permeable. Prisoners shore up their defences within the prison regime in order to survive; psychotherapy invites a less defended position, an opportunity to question "survival" tactics, and asks "at what price survival" if a "dog-eat-dog" attitude prevails? Prison is concrete in substance, manner, and attitude; psychotherapy attempts to think, to symbolize, to posit an "as if" approach as opposed to a proven, absolutist opinion.

Echoed throughout the book is the obvious paradox that is being worked with when practising psychotherapy in a prison. The two are worlds apart, and yet, as is evident in the texts, each can creatively serve the other when treating individuals whose concept of being held is extremely fragile and whose grip on distinguishing between the realms of fantasy and action is tenuous. In many senses it requires "a fall" for a prisoner, as the illusion of the mindset he or she has constructed begins to be dismantled, to step down from his omnipotent position as a hardened "thug" and reveal the traumatized victim often hidden in the darker corners of an internal prison. The presence of prison officers, bars, and concrete walls along with the predictability of the prison's daily regime are for some an absolute necessity when adventuring into such unknown and unpredictable areas of their own psyches and to catch them when they are inevitably narcissistically wounded by this encounter with themselves.

In the film *City of Angels*, Seth sits on top of a high, raised building looking down at the world below, weighing up his choice of whether to remain an angel or to take the plunge and fall to earth and thereby attain a human persona. In his angelic state he gains eternal life but cannot experience human sensations. He cannot be visible to the human eye nor truly be in touch with, or express, his emotional world and feelings in relation to others. The catalyst for his decision to "fall" is in the form of a female doctor with whom he has developed a strong emotional attachment, albeit from his defended, removed position.

We watch with suspense as he, holding her in mind, summons his courage and hurls himself off the building, crashing to the ground, awakening wounded, bleeding, and disoriented. As the story continues and the tragic events unfold, we see Seth's journey of becoming increasingly of this world and in touch with a real self, as opposed to clinging on to a false self, thereby trying to stave off the pull of human emotions and experiences. In an attempt to avoid the existential crises that come with being human and truly engaging with the rough and tumble of life and relationships, Seth realizes that he is also passing up a gift—the gift to be found in opening oneself up to the sensory, feeling world of an intimate engagement with life.

People who commit crimes cannot be in touch with a feeling inner world, nor can they participate in the kind of intimacy I am describing: a close and receptive attunement to human experience and encounter with others. They often develop the kind of detachment and aloofness that is witnessed in the fictional character of Seth, their grandiosity and omnipotence defending against human frailty and helplessness in the face of circumstances and experiences that move beyond their control. The rage they carry within lifts them out of their pain and sadness, and revenge becomes the chosen currency which will always buy them a place behind prison bars.

To risk forming an attachment that is meaningful (Seth to the doctor, the prisoner to the psychotherapist) means having to face and encounter the one who is being defended: with offenders, frequently a very damaged child. When contacted, there will be a fall; coming down to earth and getting in touch with their reality will mean that wounds will be felt, the ones they have experienced and delivered. This is "bloody" work, and it will be disorienting for the prisoner, who so often inhabits a fixed belief system that—like that of the prison—is rigid and concrete.

On a recent Radio 4 documentary about prisoners serving a life sentence, one prisoner described the faces/lies that have to be maintained in prison. He said that the biggest lie told is that to families, who must not be able to read in the prisoners' faces the humiliation or despair about their predicament. The second lie is to fellow inmates, the lie of an "I-can-handle-it face". The real face, he continued, is when the door shuts, the key turns, and the mask can drop, and you think, "What the hell am I doing here?" This truth, however, is one that is rarely shown to another.

The practice of psychotherapy in a prison environment requires the therapist to venture into the hidden worlds of both the prison and the inmates and to keep alive for the prisoner the question: "What am I doing here?" In the following chapters the reader will begin to get a sense of the challenge that is present within this task. My own chapter presents some of the concrete facts about prison life, alongside some of the dynamic issues that this poses for psychotherapy in practice. This is followed by Lynn Greenwood's chapter, which describes the experience of being a trainee in psychotherapy whilst working on a lifers' wing. She stresses the importance of the support systems that the therapist requires in undertaking such work and the toll it can take on one's professional and personal reserves. Ronald

Doctor's chapter presents an important insight into group psychotherapy in prisons and the complexities that this brings. He particularly highlights the difficulties that this presents to the prisoners as individuals in terms of challenging the accepted norms of prison life, such as the subterfuge the group erects as protection around itself. Perhaps the most disturbing material comes in the following chapter, by Paola Franciosi, the only contribution from a psychotherapist working in a women's prison. In this chapter she presents the very traumatic work involved in treating women who have harmed their own children, and she refers within the chapter to the prison's collusion in not wanting to "see" the reality of what these women have done. Finally, Mark Morris presents an erudite chapter specifically about a prison institution itself, namely Grendon. He echoes some of my own thoughts about paradox and the considerations that have to be held in mind when maintaining a link between security and therapy.

Psychoanalytic psychotherapy as a practice is the antithesis of a prison regime. The difference is analogous to, on the one hand, allowing a child to discover creatively, with accompanying mess, the route by which a spoon reaches its mouth and, on the other, sitting the child down, metaphorically tying its hands behind the chair, and steering the course for them in the service of maintaining "good order and conduct". The former encourages a more playful, exploratory relationship to the world and development, the latter restricts spontaneous discovery and attempts through repression to avoid the mess. What psychotherapy within a prison is seeking to do is to foster and develop a relationship between these two: the parental figure that stands for discipline, and the other who can take up a less fearsome relationship to the child's/inmate's chaos. However, for the child to feel secure within this relationship, the parents must dialogue and gain an understanding of the role and task of the other.

Psychotherapy in prisons has a long way to go in this respect. In small corners within these institutions, attempts are being made to allow security and therapy to coexist and for each to value and uphold the importance of the other. Still, however, therapy—a world of feeling and meaning—can be perceived as a very real threat when it comes to thinking about the crimes that have been committed and the dynamics that get enacted within the prison's walls. It requires an act of courage to "take the plunge", relinquish a position of defence, and choose to "see" and be seen, as opposed to remaining hidden.

Jessica Williams Saunders

LIFE WITHIN
HIDDEN WORLDS

CHAPTER ONE

An introduction to psychotherapy in prisons: issues, themes, and dynamics

Jessica Williams Saunders

When we consider the notion of practising psychotherapy in prisons, we are immediately moving into the realms of paradoxical thinking. Imagine, if you will, two diametrically opposed views of the world. One operates along the lines of crime and punishment, a system based on absolutes and reliance on a set of rules where the notion of clearly identifiable facts can be proven or not, and where a path of retribution is laid in concrete terms by the prisoner "doing time" and serving a sentence and by seeing that justice is done on behalf of the victims of crime and in the eyes of society. Now consider the other, a land of poetry and enquiry where free association—the playing with ideas and thought—is an altogether more fluid process and one that is open to speculation. "Association" is the name given to the prisoners' free time when they are unlocked on their wings (living quarters) and are allowed to mix with each other, watch television, and generally move around the living space as opposed to remaining locked in their cells. In psychotherapy, both the therapist and the patient are engaged in a process of interaction in a psychic space, a

1

potential arena where the secret, shadow world of the offender can be gradually unlocked and illuminated by throwing light on his or her intrapsychic processes and object relationships. The criminal justice system and the process of forensic psychotherapy are both inhabiting the role of investigator, with one seeking to prove and then punish if guilty, the other seeking to consider, reflect upon, and make sense of the motivating factors that make up the offenders' core complex and enable them potentially to find their own path, one towards redemption. Within this context the prison provides the concrete holding in the prisoners' external world whilst the psychotherapist and the process of psychotherapy hold the prisoners psychologically and emotionally in the exploration of their inner worlds.

The subject area that I concentrate on in the following exploration is undoubtedly a vast and complex one. Just like those who newly arrive in a prison (whether staff or prisoner), readers could find themselves overwhelmed if presented, within the limited space of this chapter, with the full range of issues that need to be held in mind when working in a prison. By way of an "induction" to these places of incarceration, I have presented some key points for consideration. These, I hope, will not only make for interesting reading, but also provide, for those considering practising psychotherapy in a prison, a framework in which they can begin to find the "freedom" to undertake their own explorations within the prison walls. The areas covered are as follows:

- *Scene setting.* A discussion based on imprisonment and humanitarian concerns.

- *Background.* An outline of some of the provision that is currently in place for prisoners' rehabilitation.

- *Prison types and sentencing stage—implications for psychotherapy.* An exploration of the remand, sentenced, and pre-release stages for a prisoner and the differing issues that these pose for psychotherapy practice.

- *The treatment-room—where is the prisoner to be seen?* Some thoughts on seeing prisoners on or off their living quarters and some of the dynamics surrounding this.

- *Security.* The secure environment and the psychotherapist's awareness of "danger".
- *Keys.* The power of keys and some points to consider regarding their concrete and symbolic meaning.
- *The individual and the group.* An introduction to:
  a. the prisoners and the treatment modality—individual and group psychotherapy in prisons.
  b. the prison officers as a reflection of the prisoner group and dynamics.
  c. the psychotherapist and his or her position outside the group.
- *Conclusion.* Reflections on paradox and the relationship between the prison and the process of psychotherapy.

Scene setting

In the early part of 1998, Karla Faye Tucker was executed in the United States, having been held on Death Row since receiving her death sentence thirteen years previously. This act raises several key and thorny issues relevant to the nature of sentencing procedures and the role and place that physical incarceration plays within this. How is it, I have questioned, that someone who receives the death penalty then has to wait years for this to be carried out? Within this time lapse, it would perhaps seem that no real account was taken of her personal process and development, nor of the productive way in which her time had been spent throughout her years in prison. What, then, is the role of prison in light of this—is it a stronghold whose main function is primarily concerned with retribution and the protection of society, or is it one in which society's needs, the needs of the victims of crime, and the needs and continued development of the prisoner are taken into consideration? Reports of Faye Tucker's early life as a child painted a dark picture, to say the least, as is the case with many offenders; nevertheless, this is no grounds on which to condone her (or others') murderous actions, for which only she (or they) could be responsible. However, it surely bears consideration in terms of evaluating her "rehabilitation" and her capacity, thirteen years on from the murders, to link her internal world to that of the external one and to the events that took place within it that led to her imprisonment in the first place. Enabling prisoners to make such links in a way that might effect change and assessing their rehabilitative process would, however, require a fundamental shift in the way we think about offenders—that is, that they are capable of change and worthy of earned forgiveness. Such a change in perspective also opens up a doorway for psychotherapy to have a role and place in prisons and for it to exist side by side with punishment. In Faye Tucker's case, it seems that there was no room within the criminal justice system, or within the minds of those who could have stepped in, to consider the possibility of reprieve from death as punishment and thereby consider the notion of the offender's own personal guilt about what he or she has done and his or her willingness to take responsibility for such actions. If this were to be the case, it might allow the prisoner to seek forgiveness, both from those who condemn and from his or her own self-condemning natures, and for society to move beyond a punitive desire for retribution and to embrace a more compassionate response that can encompass the place of redemption.

In working as a therapist with people who have committed sometimes heinous crimes, it has become apparent that by far the hardest task for offenders is for them to think about and come to terms with what they have done and to *live* with this. Death as a punishment is, I believe, a primitive response towards someone who murders, and as such it displays the desire on society's behalf for revenge and annihilation of the offending object—the very drives that fuel the murderer's internal world and propel him or her into the acts that he or she commits. I recognize that I am treading on delicate ground here in referring to a case of corporal punishment, as the latter is no longer considered acceptable in the United Kingdom. However, I cite this particular case on two accounts: first, because whilst we may not in practice continue with such punishment, in the minds of some of the British public (and even of some people who work in prisons) the desire to do unto prisoners what they have done to their victims is still as alive today as it was when hanging and public execution were part of the penal system in this country. Indeed, for some the idea that "prison is too good for them" and that prisons are some kind of holiday camp are still firmly held views and beliefs. Second, I have witnessed the toll that incarceration can take on an individual's psyche and the kind of spiritual death that can be very real when human beings are sentenced to a life of deprivation behind bars. So whilst we may not actually take their physical life in atonement for their "sins", it is the case for a large number of prisoners that in the experience of imprisonment their already fragile egos and grip on life (often disguised as omnipotence and grandiosity) are further and sometimes irretrievably eroded. Prison can be a crucifying experience.

Far from "teaching them a lesson" in the hope of changing offenders' behaviour, prison sentences and punishment per se can also serve to confirm further to prisoners their entrenched beliefs that they are victims of a punitive and abusive world (an inner world projected onto the outer and concretized as reality), and that their anti-authoritarian stance serves their rightful need to be heard and seen. Prison and punishment thus can potentially fuel rather than change their maladjusted coping mechanisms and perpetuate a cycle in which destruction and darkness win out over creativity and enlightenment and the potential for growth and change. Therefore, it would seem that the rather naive and polarized idea that the sentence and time served in prison will, in and of itself, bring about change—or, at the other end of the spectrum, count for nothing, as in the case cited—is one that begs consideration: first, in terms of bringing about effective measures in combating crime (i.e. in gaining a greater understanding of what leads people to commit offences) and, second, in terms of attempting to make a prisoner's life in prison one that can be meaningful and productive, counting for something, and thus valued. A process such as this would call upon us all to think about the unthinkable—the criminal act and the act of incarceration itself—as opposed to buying into the prisoners' idea that they are "killing time" in prison and that real life beyond it is held suspended, like a sharp intake of a breath. Current attitudes and beliefs held by prisoners, prison staff, and society often remain unchallenged, and, as such, prison in this instance becomes a kind of graveyard experience, where thought and meaning are dead and buried in an attempt to lay to rest, by denial, the often haunting experiences that inhabit the prisoner's inner world and are inherent in their criminal acts. To undergo psychotherapy in prison is far from the sometimes considered idea of a "soft" approach. It requires of the offenders courage, determination, and a willingness to look at the roles of both the persecutor and the victim within themselves, roles that inform their internal conflicts which are then evacuated into, for example, an act of murder. Living in and with the full awareness of the wrongs that they have committed and with their own experiences of being wronged in life is surely the thornier path to tread than obliteration of these experiences through murder: murder that is carried out in an offending act such as the ones Karla Faye Tucker committed, via an act that some in society condone and justify as righteous, such as a death sentence or by deadly attacks on the minds of all by a refusal to engage with and think about why people do what they do. In attempting to make available psychotherapy in prisons, there may be the possibility that through treatment, those who kill and/or violate in other ways may be enabled to acknowledge within themselves the motivation that propels them into concrete enactment of their primitive drives and inner conflicts. This may also provide the criminal with the possibility of truly making amends, in terms of inhabiting and integrating his or her realities and acknowledging the truth of his or her own existence. Exploration of how such a process of self-examination via treatment can be undertaken within the punishing world of a prison requires us to enter into the underworld of both the offender and the prison itself.

In this chapter, I seek to explore this dichotomy—that is, treatment vs. punishment—by putting forward some key points about the practicalities that need to be considered when engaging in the practice of psychotherapy in prisons. I attempt to draw on both concrete and imaginative approaches in my line of enquiry—that is, to outline some givens in terms of the culture that exists within a prison in a factual account of points to consider—and to speculate in a more descriptive manner about the concrete and often rigid nature of a system such as a prison regime and the psychodynamic issues that this poses for psychotherapy in practice. More in-depth, descriptive accounts of clinical practice come in the following chapters in the case material that is presented. Whilst I draw on my clinical experience of practising in a prison to illustrate my points, this chapter is primarily concerned with introducing the reader to prison life and to examining the impact and implications that prison life holds for the process of psychotherapy, the prisoner in prison and in treatment, and the practitioner carrying this out.

Background

In November 1998, the total number of offenders (including young offenders) housed in prisons within the United Kingdom amounted to 69,952, with women accounting for 3,170 of these (Prison Service figures). Due to overcrowding in our prisons, 1997 saw the introduction of an old prison ship to provide increased holding capacity for offenders, whilst it also witnessed the growth of privatized industry for prison management and for the management of offenders, such as in the use of Securicor as carriers of inmates to and from the courts. The privatization of prisons raised some particular concerns about how standards and provision for offenders within the prison service as a whole would be monitored and carried out. Whilst such managerial structures have, despite some fairly entrenched harsh beliefs and attitudes in relation to society's response to offenders and the management of them, been altered and/or put in place, there has also been a shift in the awareness of prisoners' therapeutic needs. The number of substance-misuse programmes currently operating in prisons (still predominantly in adult male establishments) has been increased, and offending behaviour, anger management, and sex offender programmes operate in an increasing number of prisons as well. We can see that attention to some of the underlying features behind the criminal deed are increasingly recognized as being in need of treatment. Education departments, despite being subjected to cuts in their resources, continue to provide much-needed vocational, educational, and creative pursuits for inmates. Exhibitions such as the Koestler Award for art in prison enable both prisoners to exhibit their work and the outside world to witness the often extraordinary creative talent that can arise and develop even within the most depriving of environments. Continuing the theme of creative expression, a number of excellent theatre groups visit prisons and provide drama workshops as well as performance pieces drawing on themes relevant to criminal behaviour, underlying causal factors, and incarceration. Psychology departments in prisons also provide a much-needed resource in terms of individual counselling and group work, whilst probation departments—stretched as they are—also strive to pioneer some of the innovative group-work programmes mentioned above. Aside from the prison chaplain, a number of representatives from religious organizations of different denominations (ranging widely from Catholic priests to Buddhist nuns) also visit prisons to attend to the spiritual welfare of prisoners. So, on the one hand, we have a pretty depressing backdrop in terms of the increasing number of people being incarcerated, the growth of prison establishments, and the use of some fairly archaic responses to overcrowding, not to mention the impoverished environments that many inmates inhabit. On the other hand, however, we can see creative endeavours that continue to exist despite living under the threat of cuts and impingement of an economic and psychological kind. The human capacity for creativity and the desire for freedom of expression lives on, it would seem, even when the drawbridge to the outside world has been lifted and freedom of movement in the external world beyond bars has been curtailed.

I would suggest that psychotherapy in prisons acknowledges that some offenders do want to create alternative ways of being and relating in the world, to challenge their own fixed beliefs that frequently operate from a black-and-white, either/or position, and to express these through a wish for reparation in the face of their own capacity to destroy. In Kleinian terms, this process might be described as a move from a modus operandi that is schizoid in nature to a place in which responsibility for the crimes committed can be taken. This occurs by applying thought to one's own deeds as well as to the deeds perpetuated against one throughout life. In such working through comes the possibility to mourn what has been lost as well as to hold the capacity for life and death to be in relationship with, as opposed to against, each other.

Prison types and sentencing stage— implications for psychotherapy

There are a number of different types of prisons in the United Kingdom, and each poses different considerations, constraints, and issues for the practice of psychotherapy, as discussed below.

Remand/local prisons—these hold men and women who are awaiting trial and those who have been convicted and are awaiting sentence. They may also hold sentenced prisoners who are awaiting transfer to the prison in which they are to serve their sentence.

Category A, B, C, and D prisons—these are for sentenced prisoners, and the category indicates the security-risk factor of the given inmates. Category A reflects the highest risk; Category B may also include prisoners at the beginning of a life sentence; Category D may include prisoners who are coming to the end of a long sentence and therefore deemed to be of lower risk, as well as those convicted of more minor offences. Within such establishments, some prisons have specialist units, such as Rule 43, where inmates are segregated from the main population for their own protection or because their behaviour has seriously contravened rules within the prison. There may also be psychiatric and detoxification units, mother and baby units in some women's prisons, as well as separate units to carry out some of the specialist offender programmes already mentioned. Some of these units may employ therapeutic community principles and, as such, become sub-systems within the overall prison regime. Currently, there is only one prison, HMP Grendon, that is run entirely on therapeutic community lines within the security of the prison walls.

Open prisons—these carry the lowest security in terms of locking-up procedures. Many inmates housed in open conditions may be involved in community service schemes, and some will be attending college courses as they move towards completing their sentence.

Young offender institutions (YOIs)—these are for offenders under the age of 21, and they operate within both closed and open conditions.

The beginning—on remand

There are a number of points to highlight that are relevant to psychotherapy practice across the range of different prisons. Remand prisons pose some of the most obvious difficulties in terms of psychotherapy practice. With a largely transitory population—the average length of stay for untried male prisoners in custody in 1996 (the most recent Prison Service figures) was 53 days, for untried women prisoners 41 days—one might question whether it is ethical or viable to engage a prisoner in this type of self-exploration, given the brevity of their prospective stay. Having said this, the strain on the criminal justice system, with its backlog of cases awaiting hearing in the courts, means that some prisoners frequently spend months on remand awaiting committal and trial. This period of waiting, like a stay of execution, can evoke considerable anxiety for the prisoner, who having been suddenly taken out of the world and placed behind bars is brought face to face with his or her own guilt (or innocence, in the case of wrongful imprisonment), powerlessness, and isolation. Prisoners may also be in a state of shock and trauma when the full realization of what they have done begins to sink in. When we consider that for many offenders the criminal act itself can be an outlet for acute anxiety (just as a drug is to an addict), deprivation and withdrawal of such an outlet when they are locked up can often trigger panic attacks, which are not uncommon at the start of a stay in prison. Therefore, whether the offence is a "petty crime" or one of a more serious nature, there may be a very real need for psychic holding of a supportive nature in a remand setting.

Another important point relevant to this, however, also requires consideration, and that is the counsel that the inmate's solicitor may be endorsing at the pre-trial stage of the prisoner's remand. It is not unusual for solicitors to advise their clients to remain silent about any particulars about themselves, the circumstances surrounding the index offence, and the crime itself leading up to trial. Obviously they are concerned that the prisoner does not disclose information to another party that might in any way jeopardize the case that is being prepared to go before the court. Clearly, in such circumstances there would need to be a discussion with the relevant professionals involved as to why a referral for psychotherapy has been made whilst a prisoner is on remand, and what the nature of the contract for therapy will be during the pre-trial period. It may be that the referral is being made as part of an assessment procedure to gather evidence of any mitigating circumstances at the time of the offence, and this may be used as part of a report that would be presented to the judge at the time of the trial. It can potentially be a key factor in helping to determine the length of prison sentence or whether or not the prisoner might be placed on probation with a treatment order attached to this, or referred to a secure hospital setting in cases where there are severe mental health issues integral to the offending behaviour.

The matter of the psychotherapist writing court reports is one that may arise in relation to any prisoner undergoing or having been referred for treatment, whether on remand or sentenced. There is differing opinion in the psychotherapy field as to whether it is appropriate for the therapist to write such reports in cases where this request is made once the therapy is under way. Given that one is attempting to develop a working alliance in which there is some degree of trust, and in order for the therapy and the therapist's role to remain as uncontaminated as is possible in such a setting, writing reports on one's patients in the prison context certainly requires careful consideration. It is also important to bear in mind, however, that, unlike a psychotherapy department in a treatment setting where there may be a number of senior therapists (in addition to the therapist who is carrying out the treatment), any of whom could write a forensic psychotherapy report that would meet the court's requirements, in prisons it is not uncommon for psychotherapists to be working single-handedly—that is, they make up the psychotherapy department. As such it may come down to either their writing a report or there not being one at all. This poses a question then about what the best interests of the prisoner might be in terms of the presentation of such a document to ensure a fair trial. The timing of a request for a report obviously contributes to the dynamics of the therapy and the kind of impact that this will have. Clearly, an assessment report made before therapy has begun will pose different issues as to its aim and focus and in terms of the relationship between therapist and prisoner, as opposed to one that is made once the treatment is underway. In both circumstances, it is clearly advisable and good practice to discuss this with the prisoner as well as with the other professionals involved and to be prepared to work with the dynamics that this presents in the consulting-room.

The remand stage is frequently a time when prisoners are preoccupied with their court case, and, for female prisoners particularly, with the welfare of their children. For women who have just come into prison the immediate concern about who will look after their children is paramount. (Even when the father of the children is around—assuming that he is not, as is quite often the case, in prison himself—the mother frequently seems to hold the concern and responsibility for childcare arrangements in her absence.) In cases where there are discussions about the children being fostered or adopted (quite a frequent occurrence, in my experience), this painful and traumatic situation puts enormous strains on the prisoner, who will often withdraw emotionally at this point; even psychotherapy that is more supportive than explorative in nature may at this time feel too threatening. On a practical note, the prisoner who is on remand will be receiving visits from professionals involved in the legalities of his or her own case (and the children's cases where they are a feature), and as such the psychotherapist can expect to find a certain degree of disruption to any set time for sessions; such visits (and those from friends and family) will take precedence.

The middle—serving a sentence

The holding prisons where the bulk of the prison sentence is served can be seen as the life lived within it. Psychotherapy for prisoners during their sentence may take place within a therapeutic unit if such a place exists within the prison. Those referred to Grendon, the only therapeutically run prison in this country and an institution in and unto itself, are offered a unique experience of concrete and psychological holding (chapters three and four give accounts of psychotherapy in these contexts). For the majority of prisoners undergoing psychotherapy, it is more likely this will take place in a room on their wing or possibly in a room off their unit, such as in the psychology department or in other designated areas. Whilst working in a prison, I used to see prisoners for individual treatment off their wing in a room off one of the main walkways leading onto the exercise area. I will return to this issue of the treatment-room, but first a little on this period of time in the prisoner's life and on the environment that is home for the prisoner.

"Ordinary Location Units" is the term given to the residential units where the majority of prisoners in a given prison will be housed, with some prisons having a number of more specialist units, as listed above under the section on prison types. Inmates may be housed in dormitories or in single cells; to some extent they can choose which, depending on what is available and their current mental health (the isolation of a single cell would be taken into account with more vulnerable prisoners). These are not glamorous living spaces; they are very basic and barely furnished, with heavy doors to each cell, each with a small hole like a letterbox that can be opened and talked through and slammed shut again. The "letterboxes" can be closed with a key but quite often they seem to be shut somewhat aggressively, this sound adding to the others one invariably hears, such as keys turning in locks and bolts being drawn.

Shouting down corridors "To your rooms, ladies" is a familiar cry heard from the prison officers, whilst the calling out of windows, one prisoner to another, across the empty and desolate exercise yard to the unit beyond invariably strikes up once cells have been locked and movement around the prison curtailed. The thin slit windows in the cells are invariably stained and streaked with the contents of someone's last meal and/or bird droppings, which needless to say makes any sense of a view out even more inaccessible. The bareness of the surroundings lends an atmosphere that is bleak, cold, and hard, a barren and impoverished landscape, a lonesome abode that cries out for warmth and tenderness.

I recall a prisoner who had a cherished and ragged soft toy that she used to keep on her bed. It was terribly painful to see it sitting there; it looked so pathetic and forlorn and so very childlike. I remember thinking that in this environment it was impossible in some ways for the prisoners to allow their vulnerability to be seen and that this toy—along with a number of other softer images one might sometimes see, like photographs of their children and pets—stood in for and allowed, at least in a representational form, sight of these people's child selves. A high proportion of prisoners have been in care, fostered, adopted, abandoned, and abused. Countless of them have seen and experienced the most awful violence as children, and many have little or no experience of what it is to feel loved and wanted. The prisoner with her toy presented the polarity of such experiences: the ragged little child victim mirrored in the toy and the tough, angry inmate—now a persecutory adult whose protest screams out through her criminal acts—sitting together side by side on an iron bed in a prison cell. The emotional impoverishment and the psychological incarceration of the child now manifest concretely in the prisoner and her environment.

In practising psychotherapy in prisons, one can expect to meet both these characters—the victim and the persecutor—in the consulting-room. The environment described provides the psychotherapist with important information straight off: the institution—so often coming to represent the internal worlds of those it houses—offers up rich and vital material for exploration with the prisoner. In relation to this period of their sentence, one also has to be mindful that this is a world and environment that they may have to inhabit for many years, and, as such, being in touch with what it might represent whilst living within its concrete form needs to be carefully timed and held. What if the prisoner can begin to explore and be in touch with his or her more vulnerable side—is this survivable within this context, when back on the wing the hard edge is the one that predominates? There are no absolutes when it comes to this, each prisoner and the individual circumstances and ability to contain what may be evoked in the process of psychotherapy being different. My own experience showed me that generally one had to start with the persecutor in the prisoner before accessing the victim within. One prisoner I treated spent the majority of the therapy identifying the victim in her via a small doll that was one of a number of objects that I used in my work as a dramatherapist. "Soft, weak and helpless lying in that box" was how she described the doll, and it became a potent projection for her of the helplessness that she experienced as a child when witnessing the terrible violence between her parents, violence of which she was also a recipient. So vital was her engagement with this doll's image that one could almost see her as a child lying helplessly there before us; perhaps because of its power the young woman concerned made only very tentative attempts at internalizing the metaphor and introjecting her own projections. I have wondered on many occasions how this process might have been different and whether a greater degree of integration and working through might have been possible if the environment in which the work was carried out had been more conducive to such delicate and raw explorations. Ever mindful of her long sentence and the reality of life on the prison wing, I was constantly questioning the route that she and I were on in this work and how best to navigate it. Needless to say, this is an ongoing question for the practice of psychotherapy in prisons and for the therapist steering its course.

In terms of navigating the course of treatment during the remand and sentenced stages, treatment is always vulnerable to unexpected changes, beyond the therapist's and sometimes the prisoner's control, because the prisoner might be moved on to another prison—being "shipped out", as it is known. This can undoubtedly tap into all kinds of insecurity that the prisoner brings around sudden and unworked-through endings. The potential for such moving on to happen is very real and is a daily part of prison life. As such, this reality must be held in mind to ensure that, as far as the therapist is able, he or she keeps abreast of decisions that might be made about the location of a given prisoner and when this is likely to happen. So prevalent is this practice of moving on that it is likely that most psychotherapists working in prisons will at some time encounter the sudden loss of their patient, and thus, for the prisoner, a repetition is once again enacted of ruptured bonds (all too familiar to a large number of them), as opposed to an experience of mindful separation. Endings are never easy or straightforward affairs: chaotic and often fraught with ambivalent feelings about change and loss, they pose enormous challenges to us all. For the prisoner, anxieties about being left often haunt his or her inner worlds, and, as such, a timely (in the prisoner's mind) move to another prison whilst in treatment might also be an action that he or she has recourse to and instigates of his or her own volition. Once again, the therapist needs to be vigilant in his or her attendance to themes of loss and separation, particularly when the treatment is reaching its conclusion. This is likely to be a time when the prisoner is wanting to bolt and "abandon ship", communicating through such action what he or she might not be able to put into words.

The ending—pre-release

Whereas the remand prison is the point of entrance for the prisoner into this concrete place of holding, an open prison indicates the prisoner's exit route and transition back into the community. As such, it poses different implications for the dynamics surrounding the therapy, both in terms of the stage at which this is taking place during the prisoner's sentence and the function that psychotherapy might serve at this time. It also presents a fundamental contrast to remand and general prison location in terms of the freedom of movement that the inmate has; for example, in an open prison inmates are more likely to be able to walk to and from the treatment-room unescorted, which adds a profound difference to the psychotherapeutic relationship. It is interesting to speculate on whether the open prison might also come to symbolize a mind that is more open to thought and contemplation, with a desire on the prisoners' behalf to look back into the place whence they came before moving on to the next stage of life, as is so often a feature at times of change and transition. Whether this be so, consideration of the timing of psychotherapy and at what stage in a prisoner's sentence he or she receives this was certainly a prevailing issue that I encountered when working in a prison. In view of a prisoner's vulnerability at the early stages of a stay in prison (as discussed in the section on the remand setting), the stage of departure more prevalent in an open setting also poses its own crucial dynamics for him or her to grapple with—namely, around separation and the anxiety that can be evoked at this time ("gate fever", as it is called in prison speak). A place and experience of psychological holding as the prisoner nears release might provide as equally important a function as it does in the early part of the sentence. It allows the prisoner to contemplate the significance that the prison's concrete grip has held for him or her and what it might mean to be moving beyond its hold. It may also provide an arena where the notion of freedom, both literally and existentially, can be explored and considered in light of unconscious wishes to be imprisoned and to live within the concrete security that the prison affords, such wishes being informed by the lack of an internal experience of a secure base and thus an insecure and fragile ego.

There was, understandably, a real concern and anxiety that I witnessed about psychologically opening prisoners up and reaching into their incarcerated inner worlds whilst housed on Ordinary Location, as opposed to being housed on, for example a wing that was exclusively designated for treatment or at a point in their sentence when their release was imminent. The sense I had was that the general prison location was a cruel and harsh place, and to survive the prisoner needed to shore up his or her defences rather than lessen these. Indeed, this is a very real consideration. In terms of the start and end of a sentence, the remand and open prisons are potent settings in terms of mirroring experiences of attachment and separation for the prisoner; the arrival into a prison is usually abrupt and sudden, and the departure is frequently one that is not thought about and consciously worked with because of the anxieties that are evoked in relinquishing the grip that the prison has provided. Sudden and abrupt losses and traumatic and disturbed attachments have frequently coloured prisoners' lives, and therefore one can expect their attachment to and separation from the prison to be fraught times, both because of the histories that they carry with them and because of what it is to undergo a period of confinement such as this. In terms of the prisoners' histories, one might speculate on what dynamics are in play with the recidivist offender, who continually creates an attachment pattern through the process of being locked up and released. For prisoners, concrete objects have often stood in for a symbolic representation of a good-enough internalized parental object, so that concrete holding must needs be sought out. Psychotherapy in the period prior to release may therefore have an important role to play with the recidivist, who is caught in a web of seeking out inner security by returning to the "home" he has made for himself in prison.

With prisoners who have served long sentences, the tension leading up to release takes on an added potency. The open prison can go some way towards ameliorating some of the terrifying anxiety that can surround their release, when prisoners engage gradually in managing a more autonomous existence (as is often the case in an open setting) and movement from the prison to the community is done in stages. Undergoing psychotherapy at this time needs careful planning as to its aim and in helping prisoners to wean themselves off and lessen the dependency that they will have invariably formed on the prison. It can also serve in helping prisoners to engage with thinking about the future and a life beyond bars. If prison holds up a mirror and reflects back to the prisoners their own experience of denigration and deprivation, there is always the danger that the "real" world lying beyond the prison's walls becomes an idealized one, a distant and unobtainable horizon conjured up from a place of depression and despair. On countless occasions I heard prisoners talk about their release with an unreal sense of hope and expectancy, full of grandiose ideas of how it would be "different this time", as if their release was going to be like some charismatic renewal or rebirth. When the fantasy of the future was explored and thus penetrated it would so often burst, like a brightly coloured balloon, discovered to be only full of air and lacking any real substance. With this in mind, psychotherapy in an open prison might usefully take a somewhat more structured approach as in short-term treatments, where both therapist and patient clearly identify a focus for the work relevant to the here-and-now issues that the prisoner is presented with, as described above. Transference material in this instance is taken up quickly and as it arises, holding in mind and interpreting its significance to the agreed-on task in hand—for example, integration of and separation from the prison sentence, with an eye firmly on the future horizon.

I would like to see the pre-release courses that are held for those coming towards the end of a sentence include group psychotherapy as a mandatory part of this time in a prisoner's sentence. Psychic containment is so crucial at this transitional phase, and prisoners are vulnerable to regressive episodes that can at times be very self-destructive. As such, it may also be the case that the open prison has the opposite effect to opening up a psychological place of thought and, in fact, contributes to the prisoner closing down and withdrawing. For some, the anxiety is so great and the loss of fellow inmates and prison staff so acutely painful (I have seen and experienced the most powerful of bonds that can form in this enclosed world) that to shut down and cut off seems to be the only option and, for many, the familiar and therefore the safest way of negotiating this rite of passage. I have watched prisoners, as they approach their release, leave their packing and any goodbyes they can bear to make until they are almost at the point of departure. Then, at the last minute, frantically and sparing no room for thought, they feverishly do what they need to do, stuffing things into bags, running down corridors, and making for the gate. Psychotherapy at this time would invariably challenge this enactment of their inner worlds (who and what circumstances might they be fleeing from?) and for some, however, may feel too threatening at this pivotal time.

This may also be a time when a prisoner is most reluctant to engage in a process of self-revelation for fear of unwittingly, through the subtext of what he or she says in the therapy, jeopardizing in any way his or her imminent, desired, and yet feared departure. Given the place that secrecy plays in the criminal world and mind and the length of time it takes to work through all the stored-up, hidden areas of deception and fraud, revelation of the truth—and the timing and authenticity of it— is a key feature in prison work. Whether a prisoner is lying or not at any point in the therapy is one of the most complex areas of the work, and for the prisoner his or her capacity to deceive with the most convincing of guises is one of the most powerful cards he or she has and will play. At the moment of separation, because of the onset of increased anxiety, it is only human that tried-and-tested defence mechanisms may once again rise up and cloak the prisoner in a potentially false self, seeking refuge in the well-versed role of the criminal. To remain open and truthful and wanting of dialogue at this point in their sentence posits real hazards for prisoners in terms of letting the mask slip. If they have made it thus far, they are not going to want anything to stand in their way, unless they regress to the point of consciously or unconsciously sabotaging their own release— which, of course, does happen. Freedom can be a frightening thing and the world beyond bars also a cruel and harsh place.

Where is the prisoner seen?
The treatment-room

If the therapy is taking place on a specialist unit, then it is more likely to be the case that a room or rooms will have been allocated for this purpose. Within a culture that is known to be dealing with a process of understanding the prisoner's inner world, respect for and recognition of the need for consistency— in this instance, the crucial importance of seeing the patient in the same room for his or her sessions—may be more widely accepted and thus more reliable. However, for psychotherapists working in a prison carrying their "culture" with them—that is, not working within a designated therapeutic area—the likelihood of being able to maintain a reliable space for the prisoner to be seen in is nigh on impossible. Quite apart from the unconscious, or otherwise, attacks that might be made on the therapy through the maintenance or not of this space, there is a shortage of suitably private and yet safe (not too isolated) rooms in which to see patients. Seeing prisoners on their wings is rarely a private affair; if the therapy is not intruded upon by publicly announcing (officers shouting down the corridor) that prisoner X has his therapy session, then the intrusion may well come via the odd glance through the window of the treatment-room to check that nothing untoward has happened, or a knock at the door, or the door opening to see what's going on behind it. I have seen the compulsion to intrude, invade, break into, and steal from another's private world, so resonant of the criminal, concretely enacted by officers during the prisoner's 50-minute session. At times, the glaringly obvious mirroring of dynamics has caused me to smile to myself; not because it is humorous, but because at times the unconscious behaviour by staff and prisoners alike, in response to the therapist's visit to the wing, was so utterly obvious to me and yet so consciously unknown to themselves. The idea that anyone might be getting something "special"—that is, a private space and individual attention—evokes such envy and greed that attacks can come fast and furious. These may take the form of comments about the prisoner receiving treatment as being a "softy", or (as in this instance) by using the room at the appointed time for some other meeting, or by ensuring that during the course of the session it will be interrupted and disturbed. Needless to say, issues about the therapist being reliable and consistent evoked in the unreliable and inconsistent treatment-room, as well as his or her ability to protect the therapeutic space whilst standing up to the bullying attitude that he or she might encounter on the wing, will all prove within the treatment to be grist for the mill when practising in a prison regime.

Security

If the prisoner is being seen off the wing, then matters of security will obviously need addressing. Alarm bells (or "panic buttons", as they are sometimes known) are a common feature and will be found in most rooms within a prison. This in itself is a stark reminder to both therapist and prisoner of the context in which they are working. This security feature also serves as an apposite metaphor for the therapist in terms of needing to develop within a heightened awareness of potential danger. If the therapist's own "inner alarm bell" sounds, it might not be an interpretation that is needed: rather, concrete action may on occasion be called for if the therapist doubts his or her own safety. Remembering that prisoners are people who speak through actions, their capacity to think symbolically is often tenuous. The timing of negative transference material in treating prisoners, especially violent ones, is a matter for extreme caution, not only in terms of when to do so but also in relation to the location of the treatment-room. Such work calls for the focus and absolute concentration of a heart surgeon: precision and a steady hand need to collaborate effectively with the full back-up of a trusted team. The forensic psychotherapist making interpretations can be as critical and incisive as the surgeon's scalpel: the therapist must feel and know that he or she, too, is held to hold the prisoner's response to what the therapist offers up. In undertaking such work, the need for the therapist to know that there are trusted colleagues (who are mindful of the work taking place without intruding on it) outside the consulting-room door if he or she should need to call on them goes without saying. When an alarm bell goes off in a prison, it does produce absolute commitment from all; it is taken very seriously despite the number of "false alarms" that occur, and prison officers can be seen to spring into action. The therapist needs to be just as mindful and responsive to his or her internal alarm (attending to what may trigger his or her own panic) and, in concrete terms, ensure that he or she is placed strategically near to the bell in the treatment-room in the event that might be necessary to use it.

When I used to see patients some distance from their wings, whilst attentive to security factors I was aware of a qualitative difference in the feel to the sessions; there was a sense of the integrity of the therapeutic process remaining more intact. The knowledge that the room I used was my own designated area, and therefore not vulnerable to the potential intrusions described above, undoubtedly gave me greater peace of mind. This led me to feel more secure in the consistency I could provide for the prisoner and thus the experience he might have of feeling securely and safely held in mind. It seemed important, too, for the prisoner: being out of his usual living environment appeared to allow for a greater and more meaningful depth of exploration to take place. When there was some actual physical space between the prisoner and his "immediate family"—the inmates he lived with—it seemed possible to enter into a more genuine dialogue and relationship with the prisoner. The prison wing, being so steeped in "hard-core" culture, allows little room for thoughtful and sensitive ways of relating. The dynamics about intrusion and invasion (an integral part of therapy with offenders) would undoubtedly arise, but I was not also having to be mindfully "on guard" in terms of guarding the door against unwanted intrusions. Such intrusions demonstrate that psychological matters can be suddenly and concretely enacted at any moment by the treatment-room door unexpectedly and frequently opening. However, given that the room was some way from the wing, I did have to be very alert to safety issues, particularly in terms of how quickly the room could be reached if we were in trouble. With this in mind, it is undoubtedly the case that I was selective about which prisoners I would see off the wing and which not.

Keys

Seeing prisoners off the wing presented another striking difference: the journey from the wing to the room placed me in the role of "escort", with a strong security feature. Other than in the open prisons, prisoners, unless they have earned special privileges, are by and large unable to walk around the prison unescorted, and escorts have to be key-carrying members of staff. I carried keys, and as such I could escort prisoners from one area to another. During these "journeys", my role had a significantly different feel to it: the prisoner whom I was treating became someone in my charge, someone for whom I was responsible in the context of prison security. I sensed that the prisoner and I were brought together in such moments in a relationship of both prisoner and guard, and parent and child, with me, keys at my side, representing a strict authoritarian parental role. These walks to and from the wing became a strong feature of the therapy and frequently carried a profound sense of sadness and vulnerability which stays with me today. The prisoner in these encounters was so completely dependent on me to get from one place to another that it put me in touch with how helpless and without power prisoners were in the context of a prison. Such feelings and realities also resonated with experiences of abuse that many of them had suffered, abuse that they then inflicted on their victims, rendering them helpless and disempowered.

The conflict in roles for the therapist who carries keys—being perceived as "part of the system" by the prisoner, whilst attempting to hold a somewhat more benign role—is no easy task. This was brought firmly to mind for me following a session I had carried out off the wing one day. I not only had keys for doors to adjoining wings and corridors, I also carried keys to the prisoner's cells. Returning to the wing, I discovered that the officers had been called off to another wing (the alarm bell having sounded), and I was therefore put in the position of having to lock the prisoner in her room. As a general rule, I ensured that prisoners I saw for therapy were unlocked and locked in by a prisoner officer, but in this instance I had to undertake this. Needless to say, it presented enormous difficulties in the work in terms of my more neutral position and the trust that had been built with the prisoner. Fortunately, in this case a strong therapeutic alliance had formed and we were able to work this concrete reality—that is, that I had locked her in—through. However, it reinforced for me the compromising position one

can be in as a key-holding member of staff when working therapeutically with prisoners, and how potentially damaging this
can be to the treatment.

For the psychotherapist who has keys, their presence will
invariably bring into sharp focus issues of power within the
therapeutic relationship. In a system in which all are governed
to a greater or lesser extent by the prison authority, the one who
does not carry such concrete evidence of autonomy—keys—can
be perceived to be as powerless and as dependent as the prisoner. This brings its own set of dynamics with which to grapple
in the consulting-room. Not having keys also poses difficulties
in terms of a therapist's own freedom of movement within the
prison. Not only does this present real frustrations, it also adds
to his or her concerns around being reliable; being able to get
onto the wing at the appointed time for a session is dependent,
in this instance, on others' reliability in performing their escorting duties efficiently and on all the unexpected events that can
take place and influence the smooth running of a system such as
a prison.

Another important feature about treatment off the wing,
relevant to the therapist with keys, revolves around the prisoner being unable to leave the room if he or she wants or needs
to unless escorted back by the therapist. This can potentially
present the therapist with real dilemmas: if a patient decides/
wants to leave a session taking place on the wing, he or she can
do so. Under the therapist's charge, however, responsibility for
the prisoner's whereabouts rests with the therapist, and thus for
the patient actually to leave the room (as opposed to metaphorically) the therapist has to join the patient in this action. In so
doing, the therapist may be colluding in all manner of dynamic
issues that the prisoner is bringing to the treatment—that is, a
moment of flight in the therapy or a struggle for control. For the
prisoner in this context, however, not having the freedom to
come and go poses serious issues about free will within psychotherapy—the right to a choice and some degree of control. (This
is one of the most striking differences when practising in an
open prison, where prisoners can bring themselves to and from
the treatment-room off the wing; this affords them a much

greater degree of choice, self-responsibility, and autonomy in relation to the experience of undergoing psychotherapy.) Sometimes individuals do, in their own mind, actually need to take flight; if they are aware that they are unable to do so literally, then psychotherapy can become another incarcerating experience in which they feel/are trapped and unable to move. This is yet another moment in prison life when the question of who holds the power is manifest and fight–flight dynamics can take on a highly charged quality.

I imagine that the majority of therapists working in prisons would, given a choice, opt to carry keys (despite the conflicts this can bring) to alleviate some of their own frustration and anxiety in being able to provide a reliable service. However, a cautionary word about keys: when you, as a key-carrying member of staff, go into the prison, you go and "draw" your keys (i.e. collect them). These you then attach to a chain on a belt, keeping the keys in the leather pouch on your hip. The resemblance to carrying a weapon, notably a gun, which is "drawn" from its holster not unlike a key pouch, is striking. If this analogy seems too fanciful, then consider the following. Keys are extremely powerful within the prison, and the carrying of these on one's person is a potent and memorable experience. The first time that I wore them, I felt a profound difference in my own sense of status and noticed the difference in the status that these keys afforded me within the prison, particularly with the prison officers themselves. I seemed to "belong" more, to have more of an identity within the officers' culture. Carrying keys makes you less of an alien and intruder in the officers' domain; it puts you a "cut above the rest"—that is, above prisoners (and staff) who do not have them. Keys wield authority in the prison and control and dominance over another. Staff who carry keys have the potential to form a perverse and sadistic attachment to them as a symbolic weapon and use them as such against their charges. It is therefore incumbent on therapists particularly (as other staff in the prison will not necessarily have been trained to think in such ways) to question and reflect upon their relationship to the keys that they "draw" and the position that this affords them in relation to those who are without

them. Keys should be used and carried with a mindful awareness of what they may evoke for those who are at the mercy of
their use.

The individual and the group

In this discussion about psychotherapy in prisons, I have referred to the individual prisoner within the prison and in
therapy. To conclude, I will say a little about "the individual
and the group" as it relates to the prisoner undergoing therapy,
the prison officers and the world they inhabit, and the psychotherapist then working in this regime.

The prisoners

The preferred treatment modality—individual or group psychotherapy—is by and large dictated by the prison culture and
the familial worlds inmates bring with them. Unless the therapy
takes place within a therapeutic area as described (a wing or
prison specifically designed for such purposes), attempting to
hold group therapy is fraught with difficulties. Suspicion and
mistrust stalk the corridors within the prison's walls; honesty
amongst prisoners about each other is commonly known as
"grassing" on one's fellow inmates; to "grass" on someone
brings a heavy penalty; "digging a prisoner out" takes the form
of bullying when prisoners form a gang within the group and
relentlessly scapegoat the one who "grasses them up", in daring
to speak the truth. I have seen this happen within groups and
felt the tension suddenly rise and take hold of the process when
a disclosure of such kind is made. In these moments, terror and
outrage seem to grip at the throat of the group, and the individual, now standing apart from the rest, is vulnerable to fero-
cious attacks and retribution for betraying the inmate culture of
deception and in voicing his or her insight.

Learning about the histories of the prisoners I worked with, I
soon began to realize that the families of origin that many of

them were born into were the breeding ground for such ways of being and acting. Deception, secrecy, corruption, conspiracy, and the denial of reality keep these families together psychologically and emotionally (even when living apart) in a stranglehold. The grip they continue to have on an individual is profound, and, in the prison group, where an individual's family members are brought to life through the transference, members are confronted with their own historical patterns of relating, both through witnessing other members grappling with their own projections and by seeing themselves reflected in the projections of another. They begin to see their own family dramas re-enacted within the group arena. Working with these dynamics in attempting to lessen the hold of these primary experiences is frequently met with the same response as the one who brings his or her honesty and insight to bear within an incestuous family. This individual is the one who is now perceived as lying and deceptive, in as much as he or she has challenged the "accepted" story. Much of the hysteria surrounding the group's response to the "grass" is, of course, triggered by fear and anxiety about being seen, exposed, and ultimately vulnerable when the truth is out. For many prisoners, the notion of trust, care, concern, respect, truth, and compassion within a group experience is anathema, whilst transparency and vulnerability evoke feelings of helplessness and the fear of being abused. If the psychological holding is not constant during such group explorations (as on a therapeutic wing), then there are real dangers that material worked on in the group may be acted upon in detrimental ways once the inmates are back in the culture of their living quarters, when mindfulness becomes prey to ruthless ways of survival and an each-man-for-himself mentality takes over.

Practical difficulties also contribute to the resistance encountered when attempting to facilitate groups in prisons. Trying to organize a group of prisoners to be in the same place, at the same time, on a given day in the week, particularly if they are on different wings, is quite a task. The prisoners' visits and work routines and the unlocking and escorting procedures carried out by staff can all contribute to preventing the inmates coming together, as well as providing ways of avoiding what can be for the individual the frightening encounter with the group.

The prison officers

Prison officers (after prisoners) make up the next largest group in the prison, their world extending just beyond its walls to their living quarters. Their accommodation, the mess, and the social club often stand in close proximity to the prison's gate. Indeed, in some establishments the living quarters are within the greater wall that provides the boundary surrounding the prison grounds; one might speculate whether or not they too are incarcerated. Certainly, in the prisoners' eyes this is often the case: "We get to leave, they're here for life" (a comment once made to me) seems to be a general understanding shared amongst prisoners about the officers' lot!

The identification between prison officers and their world and that of the prisoners and theirs would in itself make a fascinating and, I believe, extremely important study. However, for the purposes of these closing comments, I shall say just a little on how this might relate to their capacity to empathize as individuals with prisoners, and the impact that this can have on the officers as a group.

I met a number of officers who, whilst carrying out their job, were very mindful of the prisoners' needs; some were quite exceptional in their skill at diffusing highly charged situations with prisoners, as well as in forming empathic relationships in which they managed to hold the paradox of providing security with a "listening ear", with a fair degree of trust and respect on both sides. I have pondered on this, and on the courage and ability they showed at times of crisis, when explosive, violent, and suicidal inmates, seemingly beyond reach, were brought back by an officer tuning into prisoners and talking them through the crisis. Yes, they are trained specifically to diffuse situations, but the skill that I am describing goes beyond what can be formally taught. My hypothesis, based on talking with and working closely alongside officers, is that they do share, to some degree, the experience of being prisoners. Their world is a closed one: prison officers do tend to eat, live, and breathe the world of work they inhabit; they do reflect and mirror the prisoner-group dynamic in many respects, both on the wing and beyond. Officers who volunteered to work on the treatment wing on which I worked were required to become a little more transparent both by attending supervision and in open debriefing sessions at the end of the working day. In these arenas, I got to see beyond the uniform, the power posturing, the tough bravado of the key-swinging officer, to the human person within. Just like myself and the other therapeutic staff on the wing, they too brought their unconscious worlds to their choice of career; little wonder, I realized, that for some their seemingly innate capacity to empathize and reach these prisoners was so finely tuned. As they engaged with a prisoner, perhaps they also engaged with a part of themselves that bore some faint recognition.

The officers did, however, bring an anxiety to the supervision sessions about how they would be perceived by fellow officers: "comments were being made", they said, about their choice to work alongside "the therapists" and to engage with the prisoners in seeing beyond their crimes to their motivation in carrying them out. Some had found that they were being "singled out" once off the wing and back on the "Ordinary Location" of their living quarters. The bullying mentality can also be seen in the officers' culture: the attack on porousness and transparency so powerfully in force in the prisoner group is as vital and alive amongst officers. They may feel their own positions and defences threatened by colleagues who choose to look a little at their own responses and behaviour when working with prisoners in a closed environment. Prison officers also have to survive the system: being part of the herd mentality may at times be the safer option if they want to continue to belong to this concrete world, as opposed to standing as an individual on the periphery of it.

The psychotherapist

Thinking of the prison as a large group process, psychotherapists are required to retain their position as individuals on the edges of it—required because of the objectivity they need (like a therapist in any setting) in being able to step back and reflect upon the process of treatment with the prisoners and in order that they safeguard the capacity to think and feel in a system that studiously tries not to. In doing so, they will hopefully remain "alive" and not become part of the "walking dead", as one prisoner described herself. Being porous, they are likely to soak up and take within all the unwanted, discarded angst; because they do not belong in the way that the prisoners and officers do and because they are seen to belong to the world beyond the wall, in this large group they become the containers who will transport the split-off feelings (rage, anxiety, despair), taking such feelings with them and thus out of the prison's mind. Their place on the edge, looking in, is also crucial in enabling them to withstand the magnetic pull of these compulsive, toxic, and absorbing places, which can envelope and wrap themselves around the ones within, shutting out the memory of freedom and a life beyond. It is vital that therapists do remember that there is an exit route once the door is locked behind them, and as such they need to hold yet another paradox—that of being both inside and outside the wall, part of the group whilst firmly standing alone.

I have written elsewhere (Williams Saunders, in press) about the addictive pull of such places and of the particular potency one finds in locked environments; the charge created in prisons, so very compelling, is likely to reach the therapist who is open and receptive to such dynamics. The task in remaining an individual within it lies in being able to resist the seductive pull to become one of the "gang". No child wants to be excluded from the "in-crowd"; in prisons, the infantile wish not just to belong but to merge with the group can be very strong, and anyone who is excluded from this, or chooses to remain apart from it, holds an isolated and vulnerable position on the boundary of the group. Therapists have to relinquish their wish to become part of the gestalt even when they can recognize and identify with it. In doing so, they have to bear the pain of what it is to not belong, to stand apart and witness, to hold the projections of being the "softy" or the "grass", like the kid who is singled out in the classroom for being a "sissy" and a "snitch" because, for example, he tells the teacher about the bullying going on amongst his classmates. Therapists have to speak out and not collude with the prisoners, the prison officers, and the system itself; they have to remain truthful and not allow their own minds and actions to become corrupted and distorted by the dysfunctional group. These are very strong drives, and the attacks on any attempt to give sight to the eyes of all who would prefer to turn blindly away from their own dysfunctional state can be fierce.

In the large group that in this instance is the prison, this is ultimately the position that therapists hold for it: the diviner and the bearer of truth, the one who feels, thinks, and contemplates, who softens the hard edge of this place that is concrete in mind and rigid in nature, bringing a more fluid way of being that can follow and come alongside the ebb and flow of its life without being pulled into its current. In attempting to swim with it, heads clearly above the water and looking over the parapet that is the wall, psychotherapists may ensure that they are not flooded and drowned by the sheer volume of the experience of what it is like to be an "inmate" in this most extraordinary of worlds.

Working as a psychotherapist in a prison is undoubtedly challenging in the extreme. My own experience spanned six years, four of these on a full-time basis—what would be classed in sentencing terms as an "L.T.I.", long-term imprisonment! In writing this chapter and in editing the book, I have found myself powerfully in touch with the memories that this experience holds: the corridors, the rooms, some of the faces both of inmates and of officers, some of the scenes I witnessed, have all resurfaced as vibrantly as if I had been there only yesterday. I comment on this in making the following point. Undertaking such work and holding a receptive position on the edge will penetrate deeply; it will seep into psychotherapist's whole being, as the life scripts of the prisoners and the arid landscape of the prison stir up the maps of his or her own interior world.

Whilst as professionals we may one day elect to leave behind the emotional poverty, deprivation, and cruelty that one encounters within the prison, what has been seen and heard, the feelings and the images, will continue to echo and resonate; the day-to-day engagement can be relinquished (sometimes, however, with great difficulty), and we can choose to hand over our keys and walk finally beyond the wall, but the memories and all that these evoke stay with us for life.

I believe that the prisoner is right in asking why professionals voluntarily bring themselves to such places of confinement. As psychotherapists, we need to ask and keep on asking ourselves the self-same question. In the process of doing so, we may also keep alive an enquiring mind that asks "why is anyone here?" and a mind that can tolerate the unquestionably painful response.

Conclusion

This chapter has been concerned with providing the reader with a flavour of life in prison, with particular reference to some of the features that the psychotherapist will need to keep in mind when engaging in clinical practice. Concrete facts have been presented alongside more descriptive contemplations about the dynamic aspects of what the givens may represent. It will be evident from this that holding the paradox of psychotherapy in prison can be fraught with tremendous difficulties and frustrations. Some would go further and say that it is dangerous for prisoners to undergo psychotherapy in prisons, the argument being that prisons are neither designed nor operated to function therapeutically and therefore opening prisoners up and leaving them vulnerable in this harsh world is ethically unsound. I do not for one moment underestimate the very delicate nature of such work and the skill and professional integrity that needs to be brought to it, nor do I think that such ethical considerations are without their place. However, whilst it is absolutely right to question whether the environment and culture of a prison is a "safe" place in which to venture into the prisoner's inner world, and whether it is actually possible to hold the paradox that therapy and incarceration present, I also came to believe during my "time inside" that psychotherapy, providing a place in which to think and explore, was an absolute necessity for the prisoner who wanted to use it, a necessity in counteracting the dynamic so alive in prisons of evacuating thought through deed, and necessary in attempting to lessen the chances of these impoverished and aggressive individuals repeating patterns in causing further harm and pain to others.

The ultimate paradox that confirmed my belief is perhaps described best in the following vignette.

A woman was sitting in group psychotherapy one morning. She wielded a lot of power both within the prison and within the underworld of the drug culture that she inhabited outside it. She could be cruel, manipulative, and violent. She had a big laugh that could turn like a flick-knife, suddenly and threateningly, into a steely, cold stare that could pierce even the hardest of fronts. She was known to be a "gang leader" and thus could skilfully influence and control her entire wing and beyond with barely the surface being ruffled; this was the work of an "undercover agent", a role she was adept at playing. Thus it would be true to say that transparency and vulnerability, being in touch with a soft and porous self, was not in her nature.

However, she had referred herself to the treatment wing and did, over a period of time, do some quite remarkable, for her, work. On the day in question she began to talk about her "need" to be pregnant. She had had five children already and wanted more (not that she wanted or knew how to parent these children), but the actual process of pregnancy itself brought her alive; in a sense, she could only feel alive when she had an actual (concrete) life growing within her. She described the tragic day when she found that her first-born child (a boy, the rest had been girls) was dead in his cot. I will not go into all the surrounding factors in this case, but she had had a brother who had also died, which had left her deeply bereft (and alone and helpless with an abusive father). She identified her desire for revenge for both these cards that life had dealt her, and she began to be in touch with the grief of these losses. She described walking up to the cot and seeing the dead, lifeless baby (the longed-for replacement brother), and, as she did so, her body started to heave with the most terrible crying and sobbing. She howled like a wounded animal, and the sound of the pain was as if it were coming from some deeply buried place within her. I will never forget this moment, nor have I yet witnessed in another pain quite like it. In time, working this through, she spoke about the release that she had begun to experience having been able to start speaking about a feeling world that she had locked away behind the armour of her criminal persona.

The paradox I am describing is this: for this woman and for many others I met and worked with, the concrete holding of the prison provides the feeling of safety they need to find a release from the psychological and emotional incarceration they experience. The woman described above said, many months later, that had she not been in prison she might not have begun to address such issues: "I needed to feel tightly held", she said, referring to the prison walls. Psychotherapy in a prison offers a more benign form of holding—for this woman, hopefully more like the arms of a strong and compassionate parent around a distraught and angry child. The iron grip and the loving arms, whilst seemingly polar opposites, may be able to link and together provide for the individual prisoner, who is both the "tough angry inmate" and the "ragged child victim", the very paradox he or she needs when encountering and experiencing the other.

It is my belief that it is possible to work effectively and creatively with the paradoxical issues present when practising psychotherapy in prisons, and to do so safely within a secure frame that is both concrete and psychological in nature. Without psychotherapy having a role in such desolate places, darkness would threaten to obliterate the light and prisons could become even more damaging and dead abodes for all who enter the gates. If thought cannot have life within these hidden worlds, if prisoners cannot be helped to become conscious of

their own guilt, responsibility, and losses, if acceptance and forgiveness are not upheld as possibilities, then prisons do become
underworlds without meaning and hope. As such, there is no
room for redemption, whilst night and the unconscious reign
over day and a time of awakening.

CHAPTER TWO

Psychotherapy in prison: the ultimate container?

Lynn Greenwood

E
scorted along seemingly interminable corridors and through gate after gate by a member of staff, I have no keys: my release depends on the goodwill—and authority—of someone else. I can ask to be let out of the prison; my clients cannot. Most of them are on E Wing, which accommodates "lifers". E Wing is an induction wing; here some 180 inmates serve the first few years of a sentence that may span well over a decade.

I needed a two-year clinical placement as part of my Regent's College MA in Psychotherapy & Counselling and to qualify for UKCP registration. During an earlier qualification, I had worked for 18 months as part of the student counselling service at London's City Lit. During this time, I saw a production of *Guys and Dolls* at HMP Wandsworth given by a cast of professionals and inmates. I decided then that I wanted to practise in a prison; three years later, I saw my first patient at Wormwood Scrubs.

In my "consulting-room", there are constant reminders of where I am: the clanging of keys in locks, the noise of gates crashing shut, a stream of tannoyed announcements, shrill birdsong (the inmates' pets seem to thrive in this environment) . . . the noises of everyday life on the wing punctuate my sessions, sometimes making it impossible for my patient and I to hear one another.

Background to psychotherapy in Wormwood Scrubs

Unlike some other prisons, Wormwood Scrubs does not have a "formal" psychotherapy and counselling resource. (Some of the issues discussed in this paper pertain specifically to this institution; others apply more broadly.) In early 1996, Principal Psychologist Margaret Smith started the recruitment of what is now a team of 14, voluntary or funded, psychotherapists and counsellors. Their orientation and levels of experience vary greatly. Some are humanistic; others psychoanalytic. Some are trainees with basic counselling skills who are undertaking the 100 hours' practice required for an initial qualification; others are qualified psychotherapists with many hundreds of hours' experience under their belt.

In building the team, Mrs Smith gauges carefully applicants' responses both to the prison and the prisoners. It is a challenging environment with a patient group whose life experiences are more extreme than most others. The prison does not provide supervision; practitioners are required to make their own arrangements—and must provide evidence that they have done so.

Patient referrals come from several sources, including prison officers, probation officers, and chaplains. Sometimes a review board recommends that an inmate should receive psychotherapy. Increasingly, as the service becomes more established, inmates self-refer. Without keys, it is difficult for therapists to get from one wing to another. Therefore, most see patients (usually convicted murderers) on E wing. (I spend one half-day on E Wing and another elsewhere in the prison.)

The frame

Robert Langs (1979) has emphasized the importance of a secure therapeutic setting. Broadly, this is defined as a frame supported by ground rules which, as summarized by Cheifetz (1984, p. 216), include:

1. total confidentiality;
2. privacy;
3. predictability and consistency, manifested in a set fee, location, time, and length for all sessions;
4. therapist neutrality;
5. therapist anonymity.

Seeing patients in a room off a wing means that day-to-day activities impinge on the psychotherapeutic work. The prison officers' main responsibility is to ensure the smooth running of the wing: their concept of a secure and holding environment has different connotations to mine. It is difficult to maintain conventional boundaries, a difficulty that has a significant impact on the first three of Langs' conditions for a secure frame. (Therapist neutrality and anonymity are relatively unaffected.)

Confidentiality

During the first session with an inmate, I explain that what we discuss remains between us. However, we are in an environment where his behaviour is monitored constantly and documented in reports: confidentiality is an unfamiliar concept and one that is generally mistrusted. Patients often pepper their conversation with what they *think* I want to hear—in short, what shows them in a good light: "I'm really looking at my anger problem. I'll never explode like that again." It sometimes takes a long time before an inmate will throw away these "scripts"; he needs to start to understand the process and trust me enough to explore his real fears and feelings.

This mistrust may be exacerbated when I prepare a report for a review board. Such reports are not compulsory and, in fact, are usually at the patient's request: he may feel that the work undertaken in therapy demonstrates progress (in terms of exploring the reasons behind his crime and addressing the risk factors that may cause him to re-offend). However, my preparation of such a report and subsequent attendance of the board brings the question of confidentiality into sharp relief: I step outside of the therapy room and become part of the system.

I attended and submitted a report for A's board (at his request). A report prepared by someone else enraged him. Furthermore, he felt that some of the board's recommendations did not take his real needs into account. Three weeks later, he told me that this session was likely to be our last:

A: I'm not getting what I need here, and I feel I need to move on. I've gone through my past—I've done enough work on the past—and I want to move on to my future. . . . I need to think about qualifications and getting a job. I've been applying for jobs here all the time but they haven't given me one. I'm not getting what I need here. I need opinions . . . something back . . . I need conversation. I need feedback; I want you to *give* me something.

I suggested that perhaps A was angry because I had stepped out of our confidential sessions, become part of a "depriving" system—and maybe even not represented him well enough at his board. His response indicated that, consciously, he did not believe that this was the case but, unconsciously, the boundaries between me and institutional procedures had dissolved:

A: No; it's got nothing to do with that. *This system.* I know all about *this system.* They're supposed to educate and rehabilitate you but they don't. What happens here is not right.

The sharp denial, followed without pause by an attack on the system, suggests that A sees me as part of a critical and judgmental group—the board. For the first time, I had moved outside of our one-to-one encounters and become an indistinguishable part of the institution—one that has served him badly and deprived him of what he most needed.

My role is a strange one: I am and am not part of the prison system; one of the challenges I face is to build up enough trust with my patients to overcome their suspicion of my ambiguous role.

Privacy

Privacy is relative: standards that would be considered sacrosanct in a conventional psychotherapeutic setting cannot apply in the setting in which I work. When a session is due to start, a tannoyed message—heard all over the wing—requests that the prisoner be unlocked to come "for counselling". Therapy is conducted in a room with a window in the door: to provide some privacy, I try to arrange the chairs so that anyone looking through the window sees me rather than my patient. On one occasion, where there was no window, I was asked to leave the door open throughout the session. This is not a "privacy culture": anyone wanting to talk to me or to my patient will knock and enter.

One significant result of the lack of privacy is that my patients generally know the identities of the other men I see. This has a considerable impact on the therapeutic process. With some men (arguably with all of them), it creates "sibling rivalry".

A couple of sessions after speaking disparagingly about another patient, X, B told me that he wanted to stop therapy. He went on to tell me tell that a friend who visited him frequently was angry with him for deciding to give it up.

B: She's one of you ... she's doing a psychology course, a diploma course. I said to her that I'd make a good case for her.

P: *I wonder if you think that's what you are to me ... just another "good case". And perhaps you're worried that the other "cases" I see here are doing "better" than you, that I find them easier to be with.*

B: I have wondered, as it happens. I wonder what they talk about: not *what* they say, but whether they have lots of things to talk about. I wonder what X talks about, whether he has lots of things to say.

C, anticipating a transfer to another institution, "backed away" from continuing to explore a particularly painful piece of material. While this was understandable, I felt that there was more to his withdrawal from me:

P: *I wonder whether you're worried that you'll leave and I won't think about you any more.*

C: It's just a job isn't it. . . . You have the other men you see.

P: *Perhaps you think that it won't matter to me when you go . . . that I'll just work with the next man who has the 2:30 slot and forget all about you.*

C: I don't know about that. At least I work. . . . I know some of the other inmates you work with and I really feel sorry for you. I talk to them and I think that you must be really bored with what they have to say. I know I am.

C was torn between his fear that I would "hold" nothing of him once he had been transferred and his desire to be my favourite "son". Perhaps he wanted to take with him the reassurance that I would miss him and our time together.

The lack of patient privacy underlines the need for me to be careful in the way I respond to material from one patient about another. It also has implications for the amount of time I spend "on the wing"—as opposed to in the "consulting-room". Inmates are not locked up 24 hours a day, and I believe that it is important to try to avoid one patient coming for his session and finding me in conversation with another: I must not fuel "sibling rivalry".

The fact that men finish their sessions and then walk straight out on to the wing in full view of officers and other inmates can mean that they avoid particularly difficult material. No one wants to display vulnerability on the wing, fearing that it will make him a target for teasing, bullying, or worse. I believe that it is crucial that I respect this anxiety rather than follow the conventional psychoanalytic convention of ending the session exactly on time regardless of what is happening to the patient. Where a man is distressed, I try to ensure that my interventions during the last minutes of the session take account of this to give him the time and opportunity to compose himself before going back to his cell.

Predictability and consistency

Maintaining a set location, time, and length for sessions is problematic—largely because practising on the wing involves therapists fitting into existing routines and procedures. The issue of a set fee does not apply: first, because the therapy service is manned by volunteers; second, because inmates would not pay even if we charged a fee. This does, however, raise questions (although I shall not attempt to answer these here). How do our patients view us—particularly within the context of other people who provide various types of support (from the Probation Office and Citizens' Advice Bureau, for example)? What is the perception of staff members of a volunteer therapist? And could this view (positive or negative) be communicated to the men (who are not told that we are unpaid)? What impact does that have? Inmates are allowed to miss work to attend therapy without deductions from their pay: how might this affect their attitude to sessions for which they do not pay? Will they value it? Or just see it as a "soft option"?

The requirement for a set location poses a problem: the few rooms on the wing available are allocated on a first-come first-served basis. (Elsewhere in the prison, I take whatever room is unoccupied; this might even be an association room, with windows along the wall and furnished with rows of chairs and a large television set.) If my first session starts early—at 8:30 a.m.

or 1:30 p.m.—using a "consistent" room is generally not a problem. However, starting even 30 minutes later means that I have to take what I can get.

In one particularly disrupted five-week period, I was in three different rooms. D reacted to this strongly. Twice he rearranged furniture (ending up almost sitting next to rather than opposite me). When I returned, in the fourth of these five sessions, to my "usual" room, I saw him hesitate in the middle of the wing, glancing towards the open doors (mine and one other) before coming in. For the fifth session, I was allocated yet another room; D's response was explosive.

P: *We are in a different room again —*

D: Yes, it's a mess. It's a real filthy shit-hole.

Perhaps this was as much a comment on my inconsistency and inability to provide a secure frame as it was on the state of the room.

Maintaining set session times can also be difficult. For a start, activity on the wing or a visit by an inmate's lawyer may mean that a session is cancelled or curtailed—often with little or no notice. My dependence on others to let me through the gates leading to the wing means that I am often taken part of the way by one person and then have to wait at a gate (20 minutes on one unusual occasion) for someone else to "accompany" me on the next stage of my journey—rather like hitch-hiking. Delays are rare but sometimes unavoidable.

An incident with one patient, E, illustrates his angry response to disruptions to his session.

He persuaded (or perhaps coerced—an example of "sibling" rivalry?) another man, Y, with the help of a prison officer (who did not understand therapeutic boundaries), to change appointments so that a visit from his solicitor would not prevent him from seeing me

The week after the changed session, I gave E the dates of my

Easter break and suggested to him that he may feel that this further disruption was another indication that I was unreliable and not available to him when I was supposed to be:

P: *When you swapped sessions with Y last week, I wonder whether you wanted to inconvenience me in the way that I sometimes inconvenience you.*

E: No. It's not like that at all . . . although I do think you could manage your time better. You should be regular for your clients and stand up to the system when people say you have to change session times.

I believe that E was angry that I was not powerful or authoritative enough to "stand up to the system" and saw the situation in terms of my poor time management, unreliability, and inconsistency. By switching appointments with another patient (particularly with the support of a prison officer—part of the "system"), he gave me a sense of the impact that disrupted or missed sessions had on him.

The unavoidable disruptions to the frame caused by the prison setting increase the therapist's responsibility to provide consistent and secure containment. This challenges my own resources and capacity—an issue I shall discuss briefly later.

The therapist–patient relationship

Consistency and reliability are key words in any psychotherapeutic work. However, with prisoners (as with other vulnerable patients) there are issues that have a particular impact on the therapist–patient relationship.

While I do not have keys, the fact is that I *can* leave the institution; obviously, this option is not open to the inmates. This is an issue of which—consciously and unconsciously—they are painfully aware.

During his third session, F told me he tried not to think about life outside prison:

F: I just get on with being in here; I try to forget about life "on the out". I did the crime and now I'm doing the punishment.

P: *Perhaps the fact that I come here to see you once a week is quite hard for you: I return to the outside world, leaving you behind me.*

F: That doesn't worry me. I know you're from the "outside" world and I'm from the "inside" world. . . . It's like being an animal in a zoo.

This exchange, I believe, demonstrates that F *does* have strong feelings about my ability to leave the prison and his inability to follow me. We are like creatures from two different worlds—the "outside" and the "inside"; in his world, his status is that of a caged animal.

My ability to come and go as I please creates an often intense fear of abandonment, particularly when I take a break. (One summer, *all* my patients asked me if I was going on holiday to the Caribbean—with its hot, sunny climate and sandy beaches, a total contrast to the harsh regime of a prison.)

In late June, I told G that there would be a break throughout August. The following week, we started late: G had gone to work instead of waiting on the wing to be called and had to be escorted back.

G: You're here. . . . I didn't think you were coming this week.

I interpreted his confusion as a sign of his anxiety: he was afraid that I was going to abandon him completely.

G: August. . . . Everything seems to be stopping in August: Education's shutting down, too. . . . You don't get many visits in here. . . . It's not like when I was in [name of institution], when my dad used to come several times a week and my mum used to come sometimes and my sisters. . . . It's further away here and you're not allowed as many visits. It's not that I've stopped looking forward to them; it's just that there aren't many of them.

With contact with his family considerably reduced, I had become G's most regular visitor from "on the out". G's confusion about the break continued. He started the penultimate session by telling me how depressed he was.

P: *I wonder whether you are angry that, after our next session, we are not going to see each other for a while. Perhaps you are both angry and disappointed with me because I am abandoning you for a month.*

G: Well, I'm disappointed . . . but then you're part of the system, aren't you? These things happen. Anyway, I thought that this was our last session.

I suspect that he found it easier to "confuse" the dates of my holiday and believe that I was not going to be there than to risk arriving for a session and have his abandonment confirmed by my absence.

However, while—consciously—it is obvious that I am not imprisoned, I suspect that my lack of keys affects the way in which my patients perceive me. I believe that, seeing that I am not totally free to come and go as I please, they may well regard me almost as much of a prisoner as they are. This creates a level of uncertainty in our relationship: without the all-important means of getting about and entering and leaving the prison, I am powerless. Not only am I powerless, I am unreliable: I cannot give an absolute guarantee that a session will start on time . . . or even that it will take place; my work depends totally on those employed formally by the prison.

Abandonment and inconsistency are two areas of concern for my patients; another is my ability to tolerate and contain not only descriptions of extreme and terrible events but also the man describing them—particularly a man who has murdered.

H was terrified that I would find some of his experiences so unbearable that I would stop seeing him. During our first session, he stressed that he wanted me to keep my appointments with him ("If you say you're coming at 3:30, come at 3:30—not 4:30"); I remarked that there were probably other things he expected from me.

H: Well, reliability and punctuality. . . . Oh yes, who looks after you? Do you have someone to offload on to?

P: *I think you're expressing a very real fear that you may be too much for me and that I will not have the resources I need to support you.*

H: The other thing I want is a "feelings check" at the end of the session so that I'm not left with anything too terrible. I want us both to say how we are.

P: *I understand that you don't want to be left with anything too painful at the end of the session and then have to take that back on to the wing with you. But perhaps you want to check that I've survived the session, too.*

My survival is a real concern for a patient who has murdered. Caecilia Taylor (1997) writes about her own work with one man:

> Therapy with a murderer can at times feel like one is treading on egg-shells: the relationship the patient developed towards me was often heavily loaded with the feelings he had had, albeit mostly unconsciously, towards his mother and father. At times, I was frankly afraid that by saying the wrong thing, I might trigger re-enactment right there and then, and I myself might be the victim of his murderous rage. [p. 108]

Therapist and client are acutely aware that the progress of therapy entails the exploration and expression of painful material and disturbing emotions. This is a considerable challenge to the therapist's ability to contain such material and the patient's fear that he will act on the murderous impulses that he is re-experiencing.

For months, J returned again and again to his terror of strangling me in the same way as he had strangled a female friend. In fact, he was also terrified that he would not survive another explosion of overwhelmingly powerful feelings:

J: She [his friend] just kept on me. That's when the feelings of rage first came. And then she . . . it was when she did what she did that the whole thing just got too much.

P: *I wonder if you're warning me about how big your rage can get.*

J: Yes, I am. (*Smiles*) Watch out! It's not that I'm going to do anything—after all, there's a door with a window there and there'd be a load of prison officers in a minute.

P: *But I think that you're telling me that you're worried that I might not survive your rage . . .*

J: *I* won't survive it either. . . . I'll do something terrible again. It's all these feelings I have. I sometimes think that I have a different expression on my face from my normal one.

P: *I think that you're really anxious about these feelings—particularly about experiencing them in here with me. Seeing me regularly means we are getting closer and getting closer to me may mean getting closer to those feelings. Perhaps you're worried that you might murder me, too, like you murdered someone else you were close to.*

J: Well, you're both women. There's *that* similarity.

For months, J was hesitant and nervous for the first 30 minutes of every session, until I had interpreted his fear—that one or both of us may not survive. After this interpretation and his acknowledgement of his fear, he talked more freely and was surprised and disappointed when I signalled the end of the session.

Acting out is one area of concern; the inability to remember committing a violent crime is related. Taylor (1997) summarizes this effectively:

Strange as the idea may seem, killing is an act that traumatises the perpetrator too, the more so if the task was particularly gory: in the following hours, days and weeks many murderers suffer from partial or total amnesia for their crime. This is often falsely interpreted as malingering, but in fact in this phenomenon we see the defence mechanism of repression. It has a protective function in that the horror and guilt of the act can be so insupportable that the offender literally cannot allow himself to know about it. [p. 105]

The inability to remember can extend way beyond the immediate "hours, days and weeks". Generally, my work with offenders starts well over a year after the offence: most can recall relatively few details, some almost nothing. While they may not remember the precise details of their offence, they are still terrified that something might happen during the session which may trigger murderousness while they are with me.

K had committed a particularly violent murder but remembered nothing about it. He was afraid that no one would believe that he could forget such a horrendous event. He found even a few seconds' silence in our sessions intolerable. He was convinced that he was an "evil bastard"—or, to be more precise, that there was an evil bastard inside him who might escape while neither of us was speaking.

K: I know that you think it's all right for there to be silence; but it's *me. I* don't think it's right. . . . I assume something's going to happen because it has before. . . . It might be all right. It's just that I'm *expecting* it to happen.

K was unable to articulate what might happen—just as he was unable to remember virtually anything of the murder he had committed. He was afraid both that I would not believe that he could commit such an offence and then forget it and that I would not listen to his warnings about the danger of the "evil bastard" inside him.

In this setting and with this particular patient group, I have found that my capacity to contain is of paramount importance. A desperate search for containment may well explain many offences (and, of course, recidivism). For some men, prison provides a secure, consistent, and predictable environment which has previously been denied to them. I, too, must demonstrate that I am reliable and consistent and can tolerate even the most disturbing material. In this situation, countertransference can be incredibly powerful (and informative), yet I must demonstrate that I can "hold" whatever my patient tells me.

Termination

In prison, it is rare to have the luxury of being able to plan the ending of therapy: prisoners are often transferred at little or no notice. I have finished a session one week and returned the following week to find that my patient has been moved to another institution.

Sometimes the approximate date of transfers is usually known (in the case of men on E Wing, for example, who are moved elsewhere after about three years). At other times, transfers appear to be quite sudden. (This, however, raises a question: to what extent do patients "forget" an impending transfer because they do not want to lose their therapist?)

The interruption of therapy without notice can be disturbing for the practitioner as well—no doubt—as for the inmate. Where I have had no notice of a patient's transfer, his "disappearance" has come as quite a shock and I must contain my own feelings of loss and incompletion. Perhaps the disruption caused by a move to a new institution masks similar feelings for the inmate; I suspect, though, that it exacerbates them.

Even where a transfer is anticipated, I often do not know the precise date. This creates a situation where an ending "hangs" over sessions.

L told me that his transfer was scheduled for November. The following session, he said that he had asked for it to be brought forward. I suspect, in reality, that he had little control over the date, but telling me that he had requested that the move should be sooner than planned indicated how difficult he found endings—particularly one without a fixed date. Furthermore, I imagine that he wanted to feel that he had some control over his life, that his existence was not totally under the control of the prison system and the Home Office.

A therapist's personal response

Some of the situations I have described are common to all prisons; others may be specific to the situation at Wormwood Scrubs, where most of my patients are convicted murderers. Setting aside what I believe I can identify as countertransference or projective identification, I think that working in this environment has considerable implications for a practitioner.

The lack of keys, the occasional difficulty of starting and ending a session on time (or even starting at all), and the unavailability of a "fixed" consulting-room sometimes create considerable anxiety within me. I have to be sure that I can contain this anxiety in order to be fully present when I am with a patient.

I have also found that if I have personal concerns of any sort, I am particularly sensitive to the harsh regime. (I noticed this, one day, when I caught myself sighing deeply on leaving the prison and walking to my car.) Not only does this give me an insight into the depressing effect of confinement (although I would argue that the prison also provides containment, often to men whose need for it is great), but it made me aware of my *own* need for support and containment in order to work effectively in this environment.

Furthermore, thoughts of these patients stay with me far longer than those of other patients with whom I have worked. I think that while countertransference and projective identification play a major part in this, this is also my response to the power and horror of some of the material I hear. For me, it is important to experience this response. I do not want to become inured to the enormity of what has happened to my patients nor to what they have done: I want to keep sight of their humanity and not start to regard them merely as "cases". That said, my effectiveness as a therapist relies on ensuring that my work is set within a broader personal context. First, I need to be able to draw on the resources and support of colleagues and, of course, a first-rate supervisor. Second, I must not surround myself completely with work and interests relating purely to psychotherapy: being "off duty"—taking time out—is crucial for my own well-being and thus for that of my patients.

Conclusion

Like many other institutional settings, a prison is not an ideal environment in which to practise psychotherapy. However, it is one where therapy is often needed urgently. Practising effectively, I believe, is a matter of taking account of the "shortcomings" of the system and—where possible—working with those within that system to overcome them. I also believe that it is the responsibility of practitioners (not only but perhaps *particularly* those working in such a setting) to ensure that they are up to the job.

CHAPTER THREE

Psychotherapy and the prisoner— impasse or progress?

Ronald Doctor

This chapter explores the possibility of working as a psychotherapist within the prison service. I discuss the psychodynamic processes involved in treating offenders, with addictive behaviour in criminality and in sexual and drug abuse, within a psychotherapeutic community in a prison. The therapeutic community provides an intensive relationship experience in which the interaction between the inmates and the staff within the prison institution are mirrored in the therapeutic community in general and groups in particular. I illustrate this with the use of clinical examples of how this environment allows the customary defences of violence and deviant behaviour to be creatively challenged in the therapeutic groups, thereby permitting new possibilities of coping with the anxieties of the prisoner. It has been suggested that the prison culture is an obstacle to the effectiveness of psychotherapy, but I argue that with the use of the therapist's countertransference a humane understanding of the conflicts can be achieved.

The prison setting

For the past two years, I have been engaged as visiting psychiatrist at a psychotherapeutic community centre, housed within a large London prison. The unit is separate from the other wings of the prison and consists of a multidisciplinary team, including a psychologist, a probation officer, an art therapist, an occupational therapist, an educationalist, and, essentially, prison officers. While this mixture does, inevitably, produce a certain tension, this can be constructively integrated within the therapeutic endeavour. There are various therapy groups: community groups, groups for drug addicts or sexual offenders, and small groups designated for more intensive work. Alongside the professionals facilitating the groups, one or two prison officers will sit in informally, often acting as co-therapists, even though their primary function is one of safeguarding security. Although the inmates are wary of their presence, in time they develop some trust in officers respecting their confidentiality. Inmates who participate in the scheme have personally applied and are subsequently sent a questionnaire and interviewed to assess their suitability to think psychologically and their capacity for change. Prisoners must commit themselves to a minimum of eighteen months in the unit and have to forgo any parole privileges during that time frame.

My first impression of prison life was on walking into the prison and being confronted with the most glaring contrasts one could imagine—not only the difference between the outside world and the one within, but, once inside, the drab, barren, ordinary building in front of me (a legacy of incarceration and punishment) contrasted with the unexpected find of the most ornate, rich, and elaborately adorned church, dedicated to the spiritual awareness of the prisoners. This extreme of "God the Saviour" versus the despair and misery of the prisoner's lot was yet another of many contradictions that I was to encounter, where the prisoner's drug-like addiction to his ecstatic states of mind would hold sway over any real search for deep transformation. The current debate about what to do with prisoners—whether to punish them or help them—reflects this duality in prison life itself, that of either harsh judgement or concern. Both become split within the prison, with discipline losing its concerned aspect, and compassion its strength, resulting in an attitude of brutality versus pathetic compassion.

These were the first of many contradictions and contrasts that I was to encounter in the prison system, and yet it is these very incongruities, which encourage splitting and projective processes to take place in the organization, that I found to be of help in thinking about and working in the prison system itself. On commencing my attachment with the prison service, I felt a mixture of trepidation and foreboding, stemming from the reading I had done of Hinshelwood's 1993 paper, on the prison under discussion, in which he stated that:

> I left the prison after three years, feeling convinced that the way psychotherapy was used by the prison was very limited indeed, but if there really was a will to get the best out of any psychological approach, then it would have to be in a very different way. [p. 429]

I too was concerned whether I would trip up on the self-same problems that Hinshelwood had encountered. It should be stated, however, that Hinshelwood worked across the prison as a whole, rather than working within a specific psychotherapeutic community setting. The latter setting obviates the difficulties that he confronted—such as being unable to find staff to provide an escort—and the problems one may encounter in locating prisoners at required times.

Perhaps the main obstacle to working as a psychotherapist in the prison lies in the prison culture itself, a culture that is formed and made up of entrenched attitudes adopted by the prisoner, within the setting of the prison, which dictate his relations to others. This self-same culture—one of macho bravado (when boasting, with pride, of the crimes they have committed)—keeps prisoners emotionally ensnared and renders them unable, because unwilling, to express themselves. Their fear, perhaps, is that to articulate their feelings could make them vulnerable and hence unable to function within the prison milieu, as there is no sympathy for weak prisoners. This amounts to a duplicity created by the prisoners, in an effort to deceive themselves. A prisoner is hard and lives by his wit, cunning, and deception. Those on the receiving end are the prison officers. They, too, are engaged in a relentless struggle to preserve and defend their image, self-esteem, and masculinity against the deception of the prisoners. In their efforts to do this, they must grossly over-respond to any slight to their esteem, or when being made a fool of by them. They must outsmart the prisoners by beating them at their own game of toughness. As a result, they are contemptuous of any displays of humane feelings of concern and gratitude.

By contrast, psychotherapists, psychologists, and probation officers who are acting as receptacles for all the disowned feelings of frailty and tenderness are consequently regarded as "a soft touch". One of my first experiences in the prison was to hear and feel the antagonism from the prisoners, medical officer, and prison staff towards the psychotherapeutic community as a whole for being a waste of time, a soft option, or a dumping group for sex offenders, the weak, and the cowardly.

Thus, on the one hand psychotherapy is denigrated and undermined, while on the other it serves the purpose of being the receptacle for softness and to allay anxiety and guilt. The prison culture enables the prisoner to combat personal guilt whereby it is projected into other prisoners and prison warders; prisoners often play on another's feeling and fears till his anxiety breaks out in a violent outburst, and thus he is the guilty one and the rest of the prisoners are innocent. Thereby, the pervasive attitudes of innocence and triumph within the prison, in which guilt and weakness are projected into sex offenders, prison warders, and therapists, provide the macho culture that prisoners aspire to. This defensive organization of the prisoners, prison officers, and psychotherapists serves a function—to separate or split the hard authority and power from the soft empathic tenderness towards others, thereby avoiding the anxiety and guilt of the criminal mind.

The prisoner's mind-set

Freud (1916) noted that it is not the weakness or lack of a super-ego but its overpowering strictness which is characteristic of the behaviour of the criminal person. The criminal feels a perse-cutory or oppressive guilt that is extremely harsh. Faced with such horrendous judgement or attack, he can only conceive of defending himself by mounting an equally violent assault on some enemy and thus project his persecutory violence into the cruel justice system—that is, there is identification with a harsh and cruel superego, but unconsciously through a process of pro-jection. This reaction to an internal enemy, self-condemning judge, or superego entails actually finding an enemy to assault in the real world. Having converted these violent beliefs into acts, the criminal gets a commensurate reaction and retaliation from others and this confirms his belief system. Criminals retain their belief that they are the innocent victims of society's op-pressive cruelty rather than accepting that the cruelty is within themselves. Were they to do this, persecutory guilt would give way to depressive guilt, which might be too much to bear. It is not uncommon for such extreme states of violent arousal to acquire an erotic or sexual charge, making the violence seem exciting and eventually compulsive, creating an addiction to a sadomasochistic relationship. In the prisoner, this is enhanced in that the dependent elements in the self tend to be projected into the sex offenders, and the destructive parts of the self are projected into other figures, which may be chosen for their power, cruelty, and ruthlessness. The dependent elements are then trapped in a sado-masochistic relationship with the power-ful aggressive elements, and the inmate may locate himself in one or the other group. At the same time, he cannot free himself because to leave would be to abandon elements of himself which he has projected. Another component of this, according to Rosenfeld in his book *Psychotic States* (1965), is that the super-ego is paralysed, in effect, by the addiction to drugs and crim-inality, and this in some way thereby eliminates the superego's influence on the ego which can be "boundlessly magnified and will become intoxicated with its own perfection and self-sufficiency" (p. 237). Steiner (1993) described mechanisms in which patients create sado-masochistic states of mind, "a psychic retreat", which provide protection from anxiety and pain. The propensity of the prisoner to present himself as the helpless, innocent victim while at the same time obtaining a perverse gratification from the domination of the prison organization ensures the stabilization of this refuge place.

The group setting

An example of this can be seen in a particular group in which I am the group leader, co-led together with one or two prison officers. There are 15 members comprising people who are in prison for serious crimes against the person, including bank robbery and sexual offences, whilst the common threads are drug addiction and incarceration. A recurrent practice is for one member of the group to be singled out as the receptacle for other members' projections.

> One such example is that of a child abuser who was asked, initially, to state the nature of his crime, after which he was subjected to a prolonged, hostile volley of questions and moral rebukes about how horrified and sickened the group felt towards his crime, all the while seeking to find a justification and explanation for his offence. They dub this "digging a prisoner out", and although someone may intervene in an attempt to stall this inquisitorial-like process, their momentum is nigh on impossible to stop. They are insistent for answers to questions about, for instance, his sexual preference, how the victim feels, his upbringing, whether he feels remorse, and so forth. This yields evasive answers from the offender, which, taken with the mood of my frustration (countertransference), lead me to interpret as follows: that the prisoners seemed hell-bent on an unproductive exchange in an effort to divert their attention away from their own feelings of anxiety and guilt and foist it onto the sex offender. He, in fact, responded to this by stating that he felt

safer in this situation in which the rest of the group were hounding him, as it was redolent of the times when his father beat him up. This sadistic persecution and masochistic capitulation by the offender enabled him to avoid what he feared most of all—confronting his feelings of sadness and guilt, and his own imperfection and helplessness when in touch with these.

Etchegoyen describes in his book *The Fundamentals of Psychoanalytic Technique* (1991) how transference of the drug addict "fluctuates rapidly and continuously from love to hate, from tenderness to the most extreme violence" (p. 199). There is an oscillation between the primitive addiction to triumphant potency and criminality and the more human qualities of remorse and reparation.

The drug addict fears tender feelings because they imply dependence and emotional surrender and thus trigger off an immediate reaction of destructive criminal hate, defending against pain and guilt and, ultimately, emptiness. Etchegoyen goes on to state:

> By opposite and converging paths, transference addiction becomes a bond in which the therapist is both drug and anti-drug; the addict can relate to his analyst only when he "transforms" him into the drug (saving and destroying); and, at the same time, the bond of (healthy) analytical dependence is misunderstood (mainly through envy) as a threat of the worst addiction. The transference conflict then leads continually to the drug, and therein lies both the danger and the hope of the psychoanalysis of addiction. [pp. 199–200]

A clinical vignette will serve to illustrate such conflict.

A young middle-class, public school–educated male, in prison for serious drug dealing, related the following fantasy to a small group that I was running: he wanted to flood the town, in which he lived, with drugs to turn all the youngsters into drug addicts and subsequently to withdraw all the drugs from the market, thereby causing all these addicts to be utterly dependent on him. This fantasy was acted out when, on one occasion, without explanation, he did not turn up for his session, leaving the group and me feeling useless, inadequate, and defeated, in not knowing where he was or why he had not attended the group. He came at the eleventh hour of the session to inform us, to our incredulity, that he had been visiting the medical officer in the hospital, as he wanted someone with whom to talk. By suddenly absenting himself, without informing us, he was ensuring that we would become dependent on him, by virtue of his absence, and in this way getting us to shoulder what were his feelings of utter defeat and hopelessness, thus enacting the addict's conflict of potency and grandiosity versus his inadequacy. I think he also wanted me to feel envious of the "helpful" medical officer, and thus, as Etchegoyen states, the addict can only relate to his therapist when he becomes the drug, whilst the bond of healthy dependence is enviously attacked.

Melanie Klein (1934) noted that

one of the great problems about criminals which has always made them incomprehensible to the rest of the world is their lack of natural human good feelings; but this lack is only apparent when in psychoanalysis one reaches the deepest conflicts from which hatred and anxiety spring, one also finds there the love as well. [p. 260]

This apparent contradiction between criminals' behaviour and their more compassionate and caring feelings towards each other would be useful were it not for the baffling and chaotic scenarios that emerge (in large groups with their widespread projective processes) and which inhibit the more human feelings from developing. I think that awareness and tolerance of the enormous helplessness, frustration, and anger that the inmates invoke in me, in my countertransference, during the course of psychotherapy, help me to understand their worship of omnipotence, cruelty, and revenge, which they feel to be superior to love and forgiveness. The addict's characteristic fear is of tender and loving feelings, since these imply dependence and emotional surrender. Self-sufficiency is idealized, and any hint of dependence triggers off an immediate defensive reaction of destructive criminal hate.

I think that there are particular difficulties in prison groups which have to be acknowledged and worked through, especially large group processes that can be seen as reflections of the prison institution as a whole, as Main (1989) states,

> where for various reasons, the members have denied, split off and projected much of their mental vigour outside themselves, occasionally into individuals but also a vague, non personal creation which they call the "group." In the presence of this mysterious, powerful "group" they will actually feel stupid, helpless and afraid of what it may do to them if they speak or move unwisely. [p. 102]

By relating to the "group", the individual of course renounces major attempts to relate to many of the individuals present as well as any prospect that he can make personalized relationships with them. This withdrawal from personal relations means that the individual is alone in the group, and, because he relates now not to individuals but to the group, it is mostly into the group as a single entity that he projects unpleasant and unwanted aspects of himself, which the "group" becomes endowed with.

Main goes on to state that the loss of personal relations and growth of anonymity results in the loss of personal feelings and experience of actual persons present. As such, no individual exists and only moral platitudes or intellectual generalizations remain. In this anonymous climate, individuals often hide behind the class they belong to; in the prison culture, inmate versus staff or, more commonly, "proper criminals" versus sex offenders. Whereas intimacy evokes great anxiety in the prisoners, the terrible impoverishment that results from lack of human contact and relationships and a life lived interacting with objects such as drugs, the criminal mind-set evokes a bleak and arid setting that protects from pain and personal guilt.

Personal viewpoints are concealed in statements from one class about another. This hiding of identity arises especially when an individual imports into the group a personal disagreement with someone whom he is afraid to confront directly, leading to paranoid class war and heated moralizing and righteous indignation, endowing the other classes with malice and stupidity, and creating a safe but stultifying stasis in which nobody exists and nothing much gets done. In this overdetermined state of stereotypy, even talented individuals may be careful to remain undistinguished nonentities projecting their good aspects and depleting themselves as a defence against envious attack.

I found somewhat surprisingly that after a large unstructured group meeting has ended, regardless of how it has gone, many members will gossip with each other and rapidly seek to recover lost parts of themselves and to re-experience others also as whole, personalized individuals. Many who are silent, paranoid, anonymized, depleted, or stupid in the large group will, once outside the group, begin to chatter and to seek feelings and ideas within themselves and to explore and express these with increasing confidence with their fellow inmates. Perhaps these same prisoners have projected their more able aspects into the group leader and, consequently having depleted themselves, regain their lost selves once they leave the group.

As an example of a large unstructured group, I relate a particular session in which I had invited two guests (junior doctors) to be present in the group.

The opportunity to allow outsiders into the prison (and unit) was not an unusual event and one that the inmates would normally welcome. The group was made up of about fifteen inmates whose crimes were all serious offences against the person, and who introduced themselves to the visitors with a short account of what had brought them to prison. This is always a little disconcerting because it presents the prisoners as some form of label, marked by the crime they committed, and little else. On this occasion, the visitors introduced themselves, and one of the group members, "Andy" (a bank robber), asked the visitor about his accent, where it was from. Although the question was posed in a jocular way, it was fairly obvious that this was a mocking gesture—to which a ripple of giggles came out. He answered nervously, "Nowhere, in particular" in an effort to evade precise answers, and therefore humiliation. Another inmate, "Bill" (a drug dealer), rose to the bait and coyly asked, "How do you feel about being here?", and tacked onto this the question, "Are you worried?", with a knowing grin as he did so. The reply from the visitor—"Yes, I feel nervous, being new in a group is anxiety provoking"—although it seemed too personalized, did at least help the group to be receptive to their own feelings. They reassured the junior doctors that they were not going to beat them up, which went some way to dissipating the tension. Seeing the presence of the two junior doctors aligned with me also provided a link that opened up the prisoners to a discussion (perhaps unconsciously) about the absence from many of their lives of a father figure.

"Dave", a bank robber, continued this theme in relation to himself as an absent father towards his girlfriend's children. He then moved on to express his anger about figures in authority. He said that he had anger towards people like social workers, the two visitors, and myself: "I could tell there was authority figures here today—there is a certain smell that comes with them, a fresh smell. Nothing personal, but I do not like people like yourselves, psychiatrists, social workers, and so forth—people who feel that they can control your life." He went on to describe how he felt that most of his adult life, mainly spent in prison, stemmed from his hatred of authority.

"Don", who was serving time for fraud, interrupted by pointing out that Dave seemed to be lumping people together into slots—for example, psychiatrists and social workers—that seemed appropriate to their outer characteristic, but "if the doctor's house was burgled, Dr Doctor could say that he does not like burglars and you would understand him saying that, while you feeling that not all burglars are the same."

I felt that Don was usurping my role as therapist (whilst also providing quite an insightful interpretation) and thereby trying to pass himself off as the authority. By aligning himself with me he tries to please and, as such, marks himself off from the group with his comments. As a result, my countertransference was to feel stuck between two stools: to collude with his "fraudulent", though insightful, perceptions or to challenge him.

I interpreted that the group's resentment towards authority and the new doctors, coupled with the need to put people into class divisions, was to hide their real feelings of sadness and loss in relation to their absent fathers. This theme of desertion was further resonated by me when accompanying, and aligning myself, with either the fraudulent prisoner masquerading as therapist or with the junior doctors. The prisoners had seen the two junior doctors and me entering the unit and at the end of the group session would see us leave, abandoning them to the fraudulent therapist.

Dave continued by highlighting his intense anger over recent events regarding the separation from his children. He felt that nobody really cared about prisoners as individuals with their own problems. He continued by expressing irritation over the fact that only fellow prisoners seemed to care for each other and their problems and that those in the community like social workers and psychiatrists were hypocrites. This led to a lengthy group discussion about concern for each other and whether the doctors really cared. Dave ended the session by stating that he felt that his expression of anger did help open the group up to discussion and to move beyond behaving artificially.

Each of the members of the group remains insecure, and even if he feels he is temporarily in favour he knows that the tables can be turned and that he may find himself a victim. Each member identifies with both victim and oppressor, and each is held in the same type of perverse grip. The grip gains its power from seduction and collusion on the one hand and from threats of violence on the other. However, I think that the group, within the unit, within the prison, has the potential to provide a psychological home that enables the inmates to be more true to themselves and to draw strength from each other in a more authentic and humane way. They begin to explore the possibility of coming alive in a safe and generous world, rather than inhabiting a deadly world by hiding behind their deviant and fraudulent behaviour.

Conclusion

The prisoner is ensnared within conflicts and contradictions, but, rather than regarding these as obstacles, the prison therapeutic community offers a unique opportunity for prisoners to begin, at least, to think rather than act. This community does offer some possibilities of working effectively as a psychotherapist within the prison system and, more importantly, of allowing prisoners the invaluable opportunity of accessing safely their more vulnerable and human sides, rather than having to rely on their criminal and deviant refuge place. It seems that this containing environment allows new possibilities of coping with the anxieties of both prisoner and prison officer, and of creatively challenging in the therapeutic groups automatic, habitual defences of sado-masochism, violence, and power posturing. While it has been suggested that the prison culture is an obstacle to the effectiveness of psychotherapy, its concrete holding may also be an advantage for certain individuals and, in fact, may offer a unique opportunity and setting for the treatment of disturbed persons. When an inmate has been on the unit for at least eighteen months and a certain development occurs, the inmate feels stronger and more supported by his relationship with good objects, so that he begins to have thoughts of escaping from the grip that the organization holds over him.

CHAPTER FOUR

The struggle to work with locked-up pain

Paola Franciosi

I work in a prison that houses female offenders. The prison holds several hundred women, about two-thirds of whom are awaiting trial. For some of them it is their first time in prison, though more often they have had a previous experience, either whilst awaiting trial for earlier offences or whilst serving a prison sentence.

The prison is divided into:

1. Eleven units called Ordinary Location Units.

2. A Health Care Centre, which comprises three wards for approximately 80 to 90 patients. The Health Care Centre is located on the ground floor of the building.

3. A mother and baby unit, on the fourth floor, surrounded by Ordinary Location Units. In this unit, women and their babies up to the age of 9 months live.

4. A young offender unit, opened in 1998, for up to forty young women aged from 16 to 21.

5. A unit where more "vulnerable" women live. Pregnant

women are located in this unit, as well as other women who, for a variety of reasons, may be thought to be vulnerable and not able to manage on an Ordinary Location Unit.

Some of the women I have seen in the past for psychotherapeutic treatment were located in a very small unit, now closed, that was kept totally separate from the rest of the prison. The women who were there had been convicted of or were on trial for crimes against children. It was felt that they were at risk of being physically attacked by other women and that for their own protection they should be separate from the rest of the prison population. Women who commit these sorts of crimes are now located either in the Ordinary Unit or in the Health Care Centre. There is an understanding that the women themselves would not disclose the nature of their crime to other prisoners and that the staff would be extra vigilant at times when information about their crimes came to the public domain—for instance, through the press coverage at the time of their trial.

The prison has a large education department which runs courses, some of them leading to recognized qualifications. It also runs activities such as art groups and sports. Women are encouraged to attend daily, morning and afternoon, for approximately two hours each half day. There are a number of "paid" activities to which women can apply; these are usually repetitive, unskilled tasks such as cleaning activities, whilst others, such as gardening, are very much sought after.

Psychoanalytic psychotherapy is a therapeutic resource available for a small number of women. The post of part-time visiting Consultant Psychotherapist was set up in the late 1970s within the medical department. There is a large psychology department, staffed by graduate psychologists, which provides the main part of the psychological therapies, either individually or in groups, along cognitive–behavioural lines.

Art therapy is available for a small number of women—approximately ten patients for weekly sessions at any one time. This is a relatively new resource as it only became available in the 1990s.

For women with a history of drug and alcohol abuse, there is a ward in the Health Care Centre specifically allocated to them for detoxification. Following completion of detoxification, women can apply for further treatment on a rehabilitation programme, which is a fairly intensive twelve-week process. Along with women from Ordinary Units, they can be assessed and then offered a place on the programme if they are motivated for treatment.

The therapeutic resources available are, on the whole, higher than in most other prisons, in part because it is a major remand female prison. This also reflects the view that women who come to prison have more medical/psychological problems than men who go to prison. It reflects as well an emphasis in the 1950s, 1960s, and 1970s on providing care, treatment, and rehabilitation in prison at the same time as providing protection for society and punishment for crimes.

The female prison population in England and Wales is approximately one-twentieth of the male prison population. There were 3,200 women and over 62,000 men in custody in November 1998.

A psychotherapist in prison

In the 1950s and 1960s, psychoanalysts like Arthur Hyatt Williams (1998) and Patrick Gallway (1965) were asked to work in prisons as psychotherapists. The prison environment was moving towards a more liberal structure, and more interest was being placed in the treatment and rehabilitation of prisoners. Though difficulties were described in engaging deprived and damaged prisoners in psychological treatment in an institutional setting, there was a feeling of being able to do meaningful work that would bring about changes in the prisoners' mental structure.

This initial enthusiasm seems to have faded, as the effect of the institutional setting was felt to impinge on the therapeutic processes more than it was initially thought. Robert

Hinshelwood, who joined a large number of psychotherapists in a male prison in the mid-late 1970s, had a very different experience of the work. He felt that prisoners and officers saw him as "indulgent and gullible" and that his work was seen as "simply making life easier for suffering prisoners" (Hinshelwood, 1993, 1996). He also felt that no therapeutic process could take place with prisoners unless changes could be brought about in the prison culture.

When I took up my part-time appointment in 1990, my predecessor in the post shared with me his view of a psychotherapist in prison: a sympathetic, supportive person for women who were distressed because of finding themselves in prison. He told me that there was no possibility of carrying out long-term psychotherapy work because the prisoners were not interested in it and were moved to other prisons after a short while. I felt very disheartened, like Hinshelwood ten years earlier, as I had believed that my work as a psychotherapist in prison would be different.

Direct work with patients

Initially, part of my work was to try to set up boundaries that were as safe as possible so that there would be a chance of therapy taking place. There needed to be an assurance that psychotherapy would not suddenly be interrupted by the prisoner being moved to another prison. The prison authority eventually agreed to hold prisoners for the duration of their therapy. As most patients were not able to come independently to sessions, I would collect each patient for her session from her unit at the appointed time. It is the patient's responsibility to be in her unit at that time. If she is not there, it may mean that she does not wish to come to her session.

To look at the crime the patient has committed is central in a psychotherapeutic treatment of offenders, whatever the nature of it. In the crime the patient reveals her internal world. To talk about the crime in detail, to get a psychodynamic understanding of it, to try to make sense of how the internal world is played out in the outside real world is the main therapeutic endeavour in the work with prisoners. In my view, unless this takes place the psychotherapist cannot be of help to his patient.

The crimes committed by prisoners referred for psychotherapy may vary from theft, fraud, importation of drugs, or arson to child cruelty and murder. Serious crimes are proportionally more highly represented in the group referred than in the prison population as a whole. This is in part due to the fact that those women spend a longer period of time in prison awaiting trial because of the nature of their crime and therefore are more likely to get repeatedly into contact with doctors, probation officers, and so forth. Some women may evoke the feeling that they need help because of their distress and/or because of their destructive behaviour whilst in custody. Other women have been referred because the nature of their crime creates uncomfortable feelings in the staff. This is usually the case for women who have attacked their children or have committed murder or manslaughter or other disturbing crimes. Rarely is a referral made because the patient wants to get some understanding about herself and to change. The women are from very deprived, violent backgrounds. They would fulfil the criteria for a diagnosis of personality disorder, often of the borderline type.

A prisoner is usually very reluctant to talk about the reasons for which she is in prison, even when acknowledging that she has committed the crime for which she is being punished. The crime is usually referred to, in a general way, as "the offence" or is given a name in which the knowledge that another person may have been emotionally and/or physically hurt is kept out, if at all possible. If "badness" is kept out of the therapist's and the prisoner's sight, then there is no need for anxiety or any need for changing anything in oneself. It is quite hard for the therapist not to go along with this. The therapist may feel totally helpless in a situation in which the patient's defences are, as usually happens, reinforced by the prison environment. The prison, like any social institution, keeps anxieties at bay by developing a complex set of defences. These may reduce the anxieties to such an extent that not only are development and change impeded, but even the institution's own task cannot be performed. These are termed "social defence systems" (Menzies Lyth, 1959).

If a patient engages in therapy and starts exploring her crime, there will be a lot of feelings and distress. Leaving the consulting-room at the end of the session, the patient must immediately face the officers and the other prisoners. The prisoner will try to put out of her mind what has happened in the session and will feel supported in this by the prison's own social defence system. The therapist will be left having to carry all the pain, the "badness", the horror from session to session and partly within the session itself until the patient becomes more able to hold onto it herself. This burden can at times be shared by the therapist with the other professionals involved. Support for the therapist outside the prison is very important, in the form of either supervision or a peer group discussion.

Work with prison staff

I felt that as part of my role as a psychotherapist I could provide a space for a group of prison officers to talk about their work and the feelings that it evokes. I thought that it would be helpful for officers to get an understanding of their relationship with the prisoners and that this itself could be the beginning of a move towards making a prison a more therapeutic—or a less anti-therapeutic—milieu. I felt that my role as a visiting consultant, without direct involvement with the prison's personnel structure, would allow me to contribute to the prison officers' training programme by offering a weekly discussion group. This, in a way, proved true, as I did manage to organize a group which was planned to run for ten consecutive weeks. The other side of my freedom as a visiting consultant, however, was the lack of any institutional power, and this made it difficult and eventually impossible to carry on providing this group, which was addressing some of the needs of the officers in their work. Attempts at organizing further groups met with problems, such as lack of regular access to an appropriate room in the training department. In my view, the lack of support from the prison structure played a major part in bringing this initiative to an end.

Can a psychotherapeutic treatment take place in a custodial setting?

These are some of the questions with which I struggle as a psychotherapist in prison:

1. Is it possible to carry out psychotherapeutic treatment, which aims at changes in the individual, in a social institution organized as a rigid social defence system?

2. Is the additional distress that psychotherapy evokes in the patient "too much" to bear for anyone while being under a harsh existence in prison?

    Clinical vignette: A young woman, plump, wearing jeans, a short top, and high heels, had been in prison for eight years for a murder she had committed in her late teens. She had received a lot of "support" in prison from psychologists and counsellors. Following a distressing event that had taken place while on home leave from prison, she was referred for psychotherapy. Therapy started, but it was quickly clear to the patient that it was going to be very different from the gentle sympathetic help she had had previously. I was felt by the patient, by other professional people, and by a voluntary agency involved to be a very cruel person who was adding to this young woman's distress. The patient broke off treatment. Sadly, she died of a drug overdose some time after release.

3. For patients with a violent history, is a prison's rigidly structured setting providing a "safer" place for psychotherapy to take place than there would be in the outside world (Zachary, 1997)?

4. When should therapy be offered? A person may be in prison a year waiting for trial—is the time before trial and closer to the offence the best time to start therapy?

Clinical vignette: A young woman, mother of two children, was pleading not guilty to the murder of her 5-year-old son. She had been remanded to a psychiatric unit for a while immediately after the crime, as everyone felt that she must be mentally disturbed for doing what she did. When she was moved to prison, she was placed in the Health Care Unit for the same reason. She talked about the death of her son with some distress, denying having had any knowledge that her actions would have brought about his death. She felt that there was nothing else to say, and she cancelled a number of sessions. At her trial she was found guilty of murder. After that, she decided not to come back into therapy. She felt that there was nothing to say, no need for it; she felt she had to "get on" with her sentence.

There had been a lot of reports in newspapers and on television about her trial, but she seemed totally unaware of it. She continued with her daily routine in a rather blank state of mind. Surprisingly, none of the prisoners around her seemed to take any notice of her or to make a link between the quiet, laborious, lifeless woman they saw and the "evil" woman who had killed her child by poisoning him day after day. One might speculate on the reasons why the other prisoners chose to join the patient in the process of "not seeing". Had they not done this, they might have physically and verbally attacked her, punishing her for her "badness". They would not have had any capacity for feelings of compassion and sadness. This woman didn't want to think because she felt she had to "protect" herself from the knowledge of what she had done. Her expression, "there is nothing to say", was like saying, "nothing can be understood", "nothing can undo what has happened". In killing her son, she had killed off a big part of her internal world which she had located in him. I felt that her murderousness or death constellation (Hyatt Williams, 1998) would bounce back onto her after a while and that, if no therapeutic work took place, she would be at risk of killing herself.

The offer of psychotherapy had taken place relatively soon after the crime. I am wondering whether it was too soon and whether an offer at a later stage might have been more likely to be taken up. Was she still in a state of shock after murdering her child? Could she be able later on to recognize her responsibility for the murder and own up to it? Could psychotherapeutic work lead to a mourning process that, in this case, would need to be life-long?

Psychotherapeutic work in custody

The patients whom I am going to discuss in the following three clinical vignettes are women who have harmed their children. In the prison, there are very few women at any one time who have committed that offence. Even though they may all be referred for psychotherapy, they represent a small minority of the referrals and of the patients whom I see for psychodynamic assessment and for psychotherapy. The therapy of these three women lasted from a few months to just over a year. Their treatment took place at different times during the years I have been working in the prison. At any one time, I would see only one patient who had harmed her child. I felt I had to provide containment in my mind for very disturbed, and disturbing, feelings and thoughts that belonged to the patient. I had to tolerate them and try to understand them until the time when the patient would become more able to provide containment for herself, as the therapy progressed (Bion, 1967). In my view, it would not be possible for a therapist to carry what is projected into her or him for more than one of these patients, particularly in the early stages of the therapy whilst the patient seems to be quite "oblivious". These considerations would apply to psychotherapists working in an institution like prison where there is no institutional support; it would be very different if the work took place in a therapeutic community.

Case history 1: Miss A

A 22-year-old woman, tall, slim, casually dressed, very attractive, was serving a 30-month prison sentence for child cruelty. Her son was found to have a fractured skull and fractured ribs at the age of 9 months. At that time, while in hospital in a coma, earlier fractures were diagnosed.

Miss A asked for help. She felt that her problems were mainly in her relationship with her mother. She was very angry with her and felt that she had been neglected by her mother as a child and criticized by her ever since she could remember. She felt that her mother was interested in her grandson but not in supporting her in her role as his mother.

Miss A's son and the tragedy that took place figured very little in the earlier interviews—"He didn't like my milk any more at around three months", "He was very demanding, I couldn't leave the room, he wanted me to be there all of the time", "He was crying all the time, I felt ashamed to go out with a baby who was crying; we stayed in all the time".

Miss A was the only child from her parents' marriage. Her father was thirty years older than her mother, and she had married him against her own parents' wish. Her father died when Miss A was 2 years old. Her mother worked and provided for her daughter; she never talked about her father. Miss A was bright and artistically gifted, but she didn't do well academically. She left home at 16 and got involved with a violent man, who was in and out of prison. That relationship ended before their son was born, while his father was in prison. Miss A got involved with another man before the birth of her son. This was a man with a long criminal history who would visit her late in the evening when her baby was asleep.

Soon after the birth of Miss A's son, her mother sold the family home and moved to another town. Miss A lost her only support, however limited, which she had in the first few weeks of her baby son's life. There was also a feeling of sadness in losing her parental home at a very critical moment. Miss A moved from a bedsit to a one-bedroom flat when her baby was about 4 months old. "I wanted to give him love. I wanted to be a good mother. I wanted to prove that my mother was wrong to criticize me all the time. She kept telling me I was not good enough. She was proved right."

Miss A said she didn't realize she had hurt her son. She shook him hard when he was 6 months old; then she stopped, feeling frightened. This happened again. She didn't slap him hard. She doesn't know what happened.

Miss A was on bail for over a year. During that time she got pregnant and had an abortion. She asked her GP for help. She was seen by a psychiatrist and given antidepressant medication. The psychiatrist felt she made a full, quick recovery.

The therapeutic process

Miss A's once-weekly psychotherapy lasted fourteen months. The therapist in the transference was a very cruel, critical, depriving object. These feelings would become even more intense and she would get in a state of rage each time her crime was talked about, when she felt as if the therapist was telling her that she was a bad mother who had damaged her child. She would complain incessantly about her mother's handling of her son, about her son's physiotherapist, about the social workers; everybody was incompetent and unhelpful. These complaints would be particularly intense in the session following the visit to prison of her 2-year-old son together with her mother.

Miss A came very regularly to her session. She chose to go back to her cell after the session, rather than "immerse" herself in the educational activities of which she made very good use the rest of the week. The persecutory world that she was inhabiting gradually receded, and some sadness appeared. Following one visit from her son, she started talking about the "healthy baby" whom she had damaged. In her mind, her baby was very clever—cleverer than all the other babies of a similar age. She felt that he was going to grow up into a very bright boy. While she was beginning the process of mourning the loss of that bright boy and coming to terms with her real brain-damaged son, there were a lot of feelings of guilt, despair, regrets. It was very painful work. Early on in her therapy, she was talking about making beautiful objects in the education department for her son, with no thought being given as to whether her son would be able to hold them. Later on in her therapy, she would talk about her enquiries about which object would be appropriate for children with her son's condition. She would follow the advice in the making of objects that her son could use.

She was very anxious about leaving prison and having to end her therapy. She was keen to have psychotherapeutic help, which was eventually arranged after enormous delay in the small town where she was living. I think the delay was partly due to the finite resources for psychotherapy, but also to the anxieties that forensic patients create in psychiatrists as well as in psychotherapists, who may therefore be ambivalent about taking such cases on.

Case history 2: Mrs B

First session: "It would have been my daughter's first birthday yesterday." She thought about the party they would have had—thought about Y (the eldest daughter).

The night the baby died she had gone out with a girlfriend at 7 p.m. It was her first night out after the birth of the baby. The baby was "asleep" when she returned at 2 a.m. Mrs B was woken up the following morning by the GP saying the baby was very ill. The baby was dead when Mrs B saw her in hospital. Her husband said that he hadn't done anything. Mrs B said: "How was I meant to know?"

She was referred for psychotherapy by her prison probation officer. The reason for the referral was that it seemed likely that Mrs B's surviving eldest daughter, then aged 2 years, could be considered for rehabilitation to her only in the event of the mother having psychotherapy. It was necessary to explore what work, if any, could be done with Mrs B: could the mother–child bond be formed again? What situation, if any, could be safe? The mother having therapy did later become a condition for any plans of rehabilitation for her daughter to her.

Mrs B was a 26-year-old woman whose 24-day-old baby daughter had died from non-accidental injuries. The fatal injury was a blow to the head. There were other injuries that had occurred in the previous ten days: broken ribs and cuts, scratches, and bruises to head, face, and neck. Mrs B was in prison serving a sentence for child cruelty. Her husband was in prison having been convicted of murdering the child.

This young woman had an abortion in her early 20s when her then boyfriend broke off their engagement. Shortly afterwards she became pregnant again. Fearful of having to go through another termination, she put the pregnancy "off" her mind. Her family didn't see it. She gave birth to the child in the ambulance. The birth was uncomplicated, but Mrs B found breastfeeding "disgusting"; her breasts were "leaking" all the time. The baby was a happy baby, and she developed well. A new pregnancy started four months later, with a new boyfriend who became her husband. This time the pregnancy was acknowledged; she took care of her eating, cut down her smoking, and so on. The birth was difficult, the baby was crying all the time, her husband didn't bring any flowers to her in hospital, nor any other present. Once at home, Mrs B felt "disappointed", felt she couldn't "bother", couldn't care for a baby who was always crying. Her husband, who had become recently unemployed, took over the baby's care. Mrs B didn't see the "burns" in the baby's mouth or the marks on her cheeks and on her chin.

While waiting for trial, Mrs B regularly visited her husband in prison together with the eldest daughter. No one in the family talked about the baby's death. It was "out" of everybody's mind.

The therapeutic process

When I went to collect Mrs B for her initial assessment interview, she was in her unit looking cheerful, talking with other women, some of whom I knew had committed similar offences, all looking quite happy. The other women said goodbye to her in a cheerful way, as if she were going to go on an outing of some sort. It felt absolutely chilling. This is a feeling I experienced quite often in the earlier part of Mrs B's therapy. She would talk about her family life, with her husband, the eldest daughter, and the newborn baby—doing things together as if they "really" were a perfect family. It was left entirely to me to "remember" that the newborn baby had died.

Mrs B had concealed the pregnancy of her first daughter. It feels as if she had "concealed" it from others but also from herself, as if she "didn't see it". I think there had been times when she had allowed herself to "see it", but these were very few fleeting moments. Her newborn baby had been crying more and more as the time passed; she didn't seem to be able to hear it, or, if she heard it, she didn't seem to be able to give any meaning to it. She didn't "see" the injuries; the ones she saw she didn't give any meaning to either.

Mrs B's therapy was a struggle in the early stage. She would be thoughtless and would try to get away with things, hoping that I would not see them or that I would join her in a sort of perverse excitement. She was in a rage towards me and the other professionals, particularly the consultant child psychiatrist appointed by the court. She felt that we were unreasonable and cruel.

The regular visits she had in prison from her surviving daughter were very important. Mrs B had to acknowledge that the child was growing up and that she had been away from her mother for most of her life. She started to talk about her ambivalent feelings towards her, at times feeling that the daughter would be better off if she was adopted, rather than her having to go through all this struggle in order to keep open the possibility of her daughter returning to her care. Being able to see that she had a choice, that she could think and be helped in thinking, made an impact on Mrs B and in her therapy. She started bringing anxieties about whether she could ever be a safe-enough mother, and she began to look more and more closely at what sort of mother she had been to her daughters. Gradually, Mrs B started "seeing" things, and there was a lot of sadness in her sessions.

Mrs B made considerable changes. On release from prison, she went with her surviving daughter into a therapeutic community for families, continuing the work she had started. Though there were difficulties in her therapy there, she was able to stay and to make considerable changes. She settled in her own community with her daughter after about eighteen months of treatment.

I think that the clear boundaries set by the court in relation to this woman's rehabilitation helped, rather than hindered, the therapeutic process. For a person who would not "see" or would not give a meaning to what she saw, having to consider the part she played in the death of her daughter—and the role of her husband, who was in prison for murder—and having to bring the marriage to an end provided a structure within which she could start to work. The "chilling" feeling that I had at the beginning of her therapy, when the patient was in a state of perverse excitement and I felt all the horror and the pain, gradually went away, and there was now a patient who was more able to think, to feel guilty, and to feel sad and despairing.

Considerable changes had taken place in this woman's mind by the end of her therapeutic community treatment. Still, I feel it is difficult to say how safe as a mother she would be over the years to her daughter.

Case history 3—Mrs C

Mrs C, a 24-year-old woman referred for psychotherapy by her prison probation officer, was serving a sentence for manslaughter of her 4-year-old daughter.

Mrs C said that X (the man with whom she and her two children were living) went over to her little girl one evening and "squashed" her. Mrs C was terrified. The following day they all went to the shops. When they came back, X hit her daughter again. The daughter said she loved her mummy, and she seemed well. Then she was sick. X told Mrs C to go and get a doctor, but he changed his mind and wanted her to make another call from the public phone to cancel the request. She went out, but she waited for the doctor to arrive. The daughter was taken in an ambulance to hospital and was dead on arrival.

Mrs C was referred because the probation officer felt that there was something very disturbing in her attitude. She seemed to be "acting" a part of a happy-go-lucky person. The probation officer felt particularly disturbed by her actual "acting" in a prison nativity play. She couldn't understand how it was possible for Mrs C to act cheerfully in a play about the birth of a baby after the killing of her own daughter.

This young woman was born illegitimate to a teenage mother who left her with her own critical, sadistic parents. Mrs C got involved in her teens with a man whom she married when she was pregnant with their eldest child. Her husband was a "flirty" man, who had several affairs and other children during their brief marriage. She worked during the marriage and was the sole provider for the family. Her husband, together with another man, killed a young woman known to him and to Mrs C. After the killing, both men returned home with their clothes stained with blood. Mrs C became the main witness at his trial for murder, under some pressure from the police who promised protection to her and her children but failed to deliver it. She was threatened by her husband's family and took refuge with a man she hardly knew. This man, X, had previous convictions for sexually abusing children. This was unknown to her, though she had a vague feeling that there was something dangerous about him. He attacked Mrs C sexually the night before her daughter died. The sexual attack took place shortly after X had hit her daughter in the evening. Mrs C says she felt so humiliated by the sexual attack on her that she could not think. The following morning she could not "see" what was happening, she felt "paralysed", unable to make any attempt at protecting her daughter while she was being hit. Mrs C stood watching, together with her 3-year-old son.

The therapeutic process

When I first saw Mrs C, she had already been in prison for nearly two years, expecting to spend a few more years unless her sentence was shortened in appeal. She felt that she had no responsibility for what had happened to her daughter. Her husband, X, the police, social services were all at fault. She was furious with me, feeling as if I was blaming her for "everything", like her grandparents who would always be critical of her and lock her up in a cupboard. Neither her mother nor any other person was ever around to protect her. Mrs C cancelled a number of sessions at the very beginning of her therapy, then she wanted to take a "break". With the support of her probation officer and a prison officer, a "break" was agreed for a specific number of weeks, after which time she would come back to her therapy, which she did.

The extent of the sadism and of the violence that had characterized her childhood became increasingly clear, while Mrs C became more able to acknowledge the comparatively more benign atmosphere in prison, and in her therapy. She seemed to have tried hard in her late teens and early 20s to move away from a situation of violence, and she settled in a rather perverse, but not so openly sadistic, marriage.

When the perverse situation escalated into the murder by her husband of a young woman, Mrs C became full of retaliatory and vengeful feelings, losing any capacity that she might have had for thinking and for containing anxieties. This led to more cruelty and sadism, and, just as had happened in her own childhood, there was no mother who could protect her daughter.

Mrs C was in therapy for about a year, until the time she completed her sentence which had been reduced in the appeal. Some limited changes took place in her personality structure, moving from a perverse situation to one in which there was some sadness and a feeling of having a "choice" about her life. At an initial assessment interview carried out several months after release from prison in her local psychotherapy service, Mrs C was felt not to be motivated for further psychotherapeutic work. The assessor changed her view about the patient's motivation at a second interview a couple of weeks later. Still, it felt more appropriate to offer a monthly supportive meeting with a psychiatric member of the staff, rather than psychoanalytic therapy.

Conclusion

The three women whose psychotherapeutic treatment I have discussed have committed similar crimes; they have either directly or indirectly brought about harm to their children. Comparatively little has been written about women's perversion, particularly about perverse motherhood. It is disturbing for society as a whole to think about perverse aspects of motherhood, and therefore these are often denied and motherhood becomes idealized (Welldon, 1988). Women who have harmed their children have often had perverse motivations in becoming mothers and found themselves unable to respond to their baby's demands, being so in need and deprived themselves. They had cruel, critical, sadistic parental figures with little or no experience of a loving, containing relationship. Their own mothers had not been "good-enough mothers" and they in turn had had very poor mothering.

Miss A struggled at the very beginning of her son's life to engage with him in a thoughtful and loving way, but as soon as her baby son started to develop, in terms of his feeding needs and in terms of his need to keep sight of his mother, he was felt quickly to become a persecutory object and she felt compelled to retaliate violently.

In the tragedy of Mrs B's baby daughter, we can look at two aspects of her mother that played a major part in the child's death. Mrs B did not develop the state of "primary maternal preoccupation" (Winnicott, 1965) which would have enabled her to identify with her baby, to be affected by her baby's experiences, and to meet her needs. Mrs B instead started functioning in a highly pathological way, using very primitive defence mechanisms that she had used with some "success" in the past. She turned a blind eye to her daughter's injuries, simultaneously knowing and not knowing the truth (Steiner, 1993).

Neither of these women, Miss A and Mrs B, had any external support in the early stages of the birth of their babies, when all mothers are very vulnerable. There was no adult available to Miss A to provide the containing function for her that she was meant to provide for her baby. For Mrs B, the only other adult available—her husband—killed the baby.

The lack of any external support played a part in Mrs C too, though she was at a different stage in her role as a mother. Her marriage had been rather perverse, although it had provided some containment. The loss of the marriage in an explosion of violence and death left her in a situation in which she was unable to provide any containment herself, and nor was there any other adult available to her. It was in this highly dangerous, uncontained state that another violent death took place, that of her daughter.

These women commenced psychotherapy in prison approximately a year after they had committed their offences. They had expected support, rather than understanding and changes in their internal world. They stayed on in therapy, until their release, with various levels of motivation and with some degree of pressure and/or encouragement from professional people. In my view, they made some use of their therapy. It was the beginning of a process of change which enabled them to feel the horror of what they had done, to feel sadness and guilt. However, a question remains: has therapy made them into safe mothers? Should that be the aim of therapy (Knowles, 1997)? In my view, this could only be explored if further psychotherapeutic treatment took place after their release from prison.

Women referred for psychotherapy in prison are, on the whole, more deprived and psychologically more damaged than patients referred to any outpatient psychotherapy department in the NHS. The female offenders' deprivation seems to be the result of deprivation that has gone on for generations. Usually, their mothers were very deprived, and before that, their grandmothers. Father's presence in a providing, supporting, containing role is a very rare experience. Fathers are either absent or they are present as harsh, unpredictable authority figures, who are themselves violent, delinquent, and abusive in emotional, physical, and sexual ways.

A psychotherapy treatment with such damaged women is in some way facilitated in the early stages by the structure provided by the prison, which also reduces the therapist's anxieties in terms of the risk of the patients' acting out. The initial stage of engagement in therapy can take a long time, partly due to the patient's problems, partly to the fact that usually only once-weekly therapy is being offered, and partly to the effect on the therapy of "life" in an institution, which is not geared towards change and personal growth. The middle stages of therapy can often be very short, as the time for the patient's release, and therefore the end of therapy, may be approaching. Often I think about psychotherapy in prison as an opportunity to start a process of thinking and change which will take a long time and which will need to continue outside prison. If it does not continue after release, the patient may quickly lose the therapeutic gains that she made, unable to hold on to them and develop them in conditions very different from the prison's environment where the process started.

Psychotherapists working in the NHS who have not had forensic training may be anxious about offering psychotherapy to ex-prisoners. They may feel unsure about handling patients who have acted out their destructive murderous wishes. They fear further destructive acting out as well as the impact of these patients on them in terms of their own countertransference. This is a real difficulty as the therapist has to be able to hold on to very disturbing feelings while the patient becomes gradually more able to think and to move from persecutory anxieties to depressive ones.

Whether the input of once-weekly psychotherapeutic treatment in prison for women who are very damaged can have an effect on their re-offending rate is uncertain. The number of women I have seen for treatment in prison, and whose treatment I have supervised, is fairly small and no systematic follow-up has taken place. As I have indicated, any further study of these questions would need to take into account the availability and take-up of continuing treatment after release.

CHAPTER FIVE

Grendon Underwood.
A psychotherapeutic prison

Mark Morris

The British Prison Service mission statement has two parts: first, to "keep in custody those committed by the courts"; second, to "look after them with humanity and help them to lead more law-abiding lives after release". Traditionally, this mission statement is interpreted as capturing two conflicting aims of the imprisonment: the task of security and custody and that of rehabilitation. In terms of political policy, there is a pendulum-like swing between the emphasis on these two tasks. The collapse of the rehabilitative ideal in the late 1970s led to more custodial regimes and was arguably a contributory factor to riots in the 1980s. The importance of rehabilitation was re-emphasized by Lord Justice Woolf's report on the Strangeways riots, which was followed by important developments in sentence planning and the management of prisoners serving life sentences. Following the Whitemoor escapes, the pendulum swung back with the Woodcock and Learmont reports, and security and the prevention of escapes became the most important task.

The concept of prison psychotherapy is a contradiction in terms. Psychotherapy is a voluntary process, a self-exploration that is usually painful and difficult, carried out in a setting where the client is free to come and go. Prison is prison. Grendon, therefore, a prison whose primary aim is psychodynamic psychotherapy, is an interesting concept, although one that has been in operation for over thirty years. In this chapter, I plan to explore the contradiction that is Grendon by looking first at the theory and practice of the therapy and second at the context in which the therapy takes place—a prison. Finally, the issue at the core of the "interesting concept" is explored—namely, the relationship between therapy and security.

Grendon therapy

The structure of psychotherapy in Grendon

Grendon prison, outside Aylesbury in Buckinghamshire, houses 240 residents in Category B secure conditions. The prison is divided into six wings, five of which are relatively independent therapeutic communities with 40 or so residents in each, plus a smaller assessment and preparation wing for 25. A community staff team consists of ten officers and two senior officers working a shift system and three civilian staff. The civilian staff consists of a therapist (a doctor or non-medical psychotherapist), a psychologist and, a probation officer.

A therapeutic community process has evolved similar to that in the Henderson Hospital—that is, with a focus on group work. Inmates have a group each morning; for three mornings it is a small group and for two mornings a large community group meeting. The small groups are slow open with eight members, and a therapist drawn from the staff team. As we aim for residents to stay at least eighteen months, the membership of these small groups is quite stable and is conducive to genuine disclosure and psychodynamic working through. In the small groups, there is the usual historical exploration, clarification, and reconstruction; the sharing and catharsis of trauma in a situation where trust and genuine intimacy begins to develop; interpretation and challenge of unconscious drives and wishes; and the recognition of inevitable re-enactments and recapitulations of previous situations and difficulties. The work in the groups is amplified by the therapeutic community environment, providing the client with forty "therapists" (fellow inmates) who carry on the psychotherapy in between the formal groups; these fellow inmates are able to challenge and ferret out evasions and dissemblings by the client with a tenacity and vigour that far surpasses what the therapists can muster. As the inmates say: "You can't con a con."

The large groups serve the function of being the democratic core of the programme, where decisions about residents' requests (for jobs or for changes to regime and routine) are debated and voted upon. In addition, these large groups are fertile ground for the emergence of more psychotic functioning, where staff are themselves brought to book for perceived failings and injustices. These community meetings are lively, boisterous, and at times quite frightening places to be. There is an emphasis on porousness of information. On the small group mornings, there is feedback to the larger community. After each feedback or community meeting, the staff group meet to discuss the material in their own small group; this might be specific issues or the current community dynamic in general. There is a regular programme of "reviews" of inmates, where their progress to date is discussed, in addition to the more formal prison work of sentence planning, parole reviews, lifer reviews, and so on.

The paradox contained in the notion of a psychotherapeutic prison is constantly struggled with by the community staff groups who have the twin tasks of therapy for and secure custody of the inmates. The therapeutic emphasis of the work is maintained by a complex timetable of staff groups, which includes feedback sessions after each small group and community meeting, meetings for the review and assessment of residents, and staff-sensitivity work.

The psychodynamic model of therapy

A psychodynamic model of criminality proposes that the unconscious becomes a vast storehouse of all the unacceptable thoughts and fantasies that a person has. What distinguishes the criminal is not the existence of an unconscious full of repressed violent and sexual material, because this is relatively normal. In the course of normal development, people go through stages of incestuous wishes as well as wishes to kill parents, siblings, and others. From a psychoanalytic perspective, what is interesting is that so few people are homicidal or sexual offenders. According to Freud, the struggle in life for an individual—and, more generally, for a civilization—is how to manage and channel the rapacious and murderous elements of personality. The perpetrator of a crime simply does that which we all have the capability (and unconscious wish) to do. The criminal enacts in reality that which the rest of us manage either to maintain in fantasy or retain deeply buried in the unconscious. The objective of therapy, therefore, is not to remove or eradicate the criminal wish or thought (because this is an endemic part of the human condition). The objective of therapy is to enable the perpetrator to avoid acting on the impulse in future. The way to do this is a long exploration of the perpetrator's mind and internal world in a psychodynamic process.

If therapy helps people who have committed crimes by enabling them to choose not to re-offend, it does this in two main ways: first, by reintegrating aspects of mind that have become fragmented and separated; second, by clarifying what was actually going on in the person's mind at the time of the crime. Therapy can explore "why" the person did it in terms of how it happened and then why it happened.

Often, an offender will simply not recognize his or her responsibility for the crime—it feels "as if" it was done by someone else. Clarifying for the perpetrator his or her own responsibility for what happened and challenging the various obfuscations that will get in the way of this recognition enable the offender to exercise a choice not to re-offend. In the structural model of the mind, the ego is assailed by unacceptable, lewd, and violent impulses by the id, at the same time as being bombarded by harsh criticism from the superego. To maintain equilibrium and sanity, the ego develops a series of defensive strategies to counter such assaults. These strategies include repression (mentioned above), denial, projection, reaction formation, and so on. People who commit crimes that not only society but also they themselves find unacceptable will use a variety of these strategies to avoid the emotional reaction. Examples of such strategies in the case of a man who has killed his partner might include repression (amnesia for the whole thing), denial (remembering but refusing to accept responsibility), projection (beating up a new inmate imprisoned for beating up his girlfriend), reaction formation (raising money for a woman's refuge), and so forth.

Psychoanalytic theory distinguishes between these defensive strategies and more primitive ones including splitting and projective identification. In splitting, it is not that the ego does something with the memory; the ego (and therefore the personality) itself splits, leaving a fragment of the personality that committed the crime and another fragment that is entirely innocent. A perpetrator who splits off the part of himself that committed the crime genuinely can say that he or she did not do it—it was someone else, another part of themselves. Reintegration of the personality is fostered by challenging the defences that prevent the person from recognizing his or her own complicity and responsibility in the crimes. The therapeutic work is an attempt to reintegrate fragmented personalities by following them through the psychotherapeutic process where the fragmentation will reoccur, and enabling the person to become aware of the split-off fragments.

If the primary therapeutic task is reintegration, the second task is to establish the "why" of the event, to begin to unravel the meaning of the crime. When a crime is committed, the police gather evidence at the crime scene. In fact, there are actually two crime scenes: the first is where the concrete act took place; the second is the "internal crime scene". If one man kills another in an argument over a five-pound bet, it seems absurd. But it didn't seem absurd at the time during the struggle—it was a matter of life and death. Suppose that the man who died had lost the bet but refused to pay, confident that the winner would not have the courage to insist. Suppose that the winner had all his life been humiliated by people who took liberties with him, confident that he didn't have the courage to challenge them. Suppose that there was one occasion as a child when he had challenged his abusive and bullying father about a bet he had won. Suppose that his father utterly humiliated him in front of the whole family and beat him for his impudence. Who did the perpetrator wish to kill? Who was it important to kill? Was it the drunken friend who owed him a fiver? Or was it the father who utterly destroyed his identity with a cruel and abusive taunt?

The incident with the father in this example is the "internal crime scene"; something about the argument with the friend in the real crime scene triggered off the utter rage prompted by the internal one. At the moment in which the crime is committed, the person is in a psychotic state; he believes that the victim in front of him is the person in his mind's eye. After the crime, the killer realizes that he has not killed the most evil thing that his mind has conjured up, but rather he has killed his friend. More importantly, the horrific memory that sparked the killing is still very much alive. It was not killed with the offence, and it may spark further offending.

The aim is to enable the patient to become aware of the characters in his internal world who are seen as evil and frightening; and to learn to distinguish these internal-world figures from people in the real world even in times of great stress. In the process of therapy, the person is likely to feel the same way about the therapist as he or she did about the person against whom the crime was committed. At this point, the triggers of the momentary psychotic state can be explored. Did the perpetrator feel belittled? Was some provocation unbearable, and, if so, what was the provocation, why was it unbearable, and why did it conjure up the image or memory of the person from the internal world that had to be killed? What happened back then that was so awful?

Grendon therapy—the prison context

Working in a prison is very different—in many ways, a "world apart". Prisoners refer to being "inside" or, when in the community, being "on the out", and, half jokingly, staff do the same. These peculiarities of culture are very striking to the newcomer but are probably lost as time passes. For the therapist in this setting, the peculiarity needs to be recognized and grasped because it has a profound effect on the therapeutic process.

The caring theme

The practice of psychotherapy is carried out in three broad settings, each with a different agenda. In the private sector, the aim of the work is genuinely up for negotiation. In the health service, the agenda is clearly set as caring; health service psychotherapists are employed to care for their patients. The third setting increasingly for psychotherapy is the prison sector. What is the agenda here? Is the therapist on the prisoner's side, or on the officers' side and employed to make prisoners more compliant and easier to manage?

"If you meet the Buddha on the road, kill him." This riddle illustrates a central dilemma for the psychodynamic psychotherapist in the health service. It is aphoristic in the psychodynamic therapies that if you explicitly want your patients to get better then it won't happen. They will apparently get better, because that is what you, as the therapist, want. You will end up with a compliant patient with a transference cure rather than someone who has made any real progress. Psychodynamic therapy in a health service whose mission is explicitly to care for and help people is a contradiction. Psychodynamic therapists are constantly trying to encourage their well-meaning colleagues to care for their patients a little less, so that their patients can be empowered to care for themselves a little more. The contribution of psychodynamic work is frequently that of putting the brakes on spirals of unhelpful caring that some patients can elicit.

The role of the psychodynamic therapist in a prison is vastly different. The experience of people detained in prison is not of care but of punishment. The client group consists not of victims of terrible diseases or abuse, but perpetrators—the makers of victims. They have been deemed unacceptable or too dangerous for society because of the crimes that they have committed. As a psychodynamic therapist, it is one thing finding the romantic life-saver fantasies of one's NHS colleagues a bit hard to stomach. It is entirely another being in a prison where a "death's-too-good-for-them" mentality stalks the corridors; where society's tabloid cry is that "death's too good for them"; and where, hearing some of the stories, a "death's-too-good-for-them" mentality crosses one's own mind, despite years of liberal woolliness. Prisons are quite brutal places by and large, whereas psychodynamic therapists are not particularly brutal people, so such institutions are difficult places in which to work. These difficulties might be part of the reason why prison is a world apart. The prison walls serve to exclude the prisoners from the outside world so that the painfulness of the culture is contained, so that people who offend society's sensibilities can be "put away" and forgotten about. The therapist in a prison goes into all this. The therapist in a prison brings all this out with their patients. Therapy in a prison setting is difficult to do.

How, then, can any form of therapeutic work take place in such a setting? This question prompts a fascinating observation. During a debate amongst staff from a number of prisons, one senior manager spoke of how bad he felt. The day before, a prisoner had been very disturbed, violent, and abusive, dangerous to the prison staff as well as to himself. The staff member with a heavy heart had sanctioned the use of a restraint harness, a somewhat medieval piece of equipment that restricts movement. In the concerned silence that followed, I proposed that this decision could be reframed as being caring. The prisoner had needed to be protected from himself, and the senior staff member, with a motive of what was best for the prisoner, had agreed to this. An even longer and more uncomfortable silence followed. Discussing this afterwards, it became clear that my comment had been a *faux pas*. Prison officers are allergic to the idea that they care for their prisoners.

Caring is seen as soft and namby-pamby. Prison officers do not care for their prisoners, they control them. This allergy to the idea of caring is quite distinctive but difficult to be exact about. It is something like the contempt that is poured by rough school children on their more gentle and sensitive fellows. In the school playground, there is usually a gender element to it, so that it is small boys who are contemptuous of small girls who have these caring impulses, who worry about injured birds and so on. Likewise, this attitude among prison officers might be conceived of as a stereotypically masculine or macho attitude. This pre-genital masculinity can also hijack the security agenda, where the necessary paraphernalia for the prevention of riots becomes fetishized. But this contempt for caring is curious given the obvious affection that prison officers have for "their lads" on their wing. Bonds develop between the two groups, with a shared commitment and identification to the wing and the prison they both are placed in. Officers put a lot of effort into the development of regimes and activities to improve the prospects of prisoners in their wings, who in a very genuine way are "in their care". The attitude has been described by some as similar to the "tough love" that the regimental sergeant-major has for his new recruits; harsh but protective. I have seen something similar from old traditional charge-nurses in large psychiatric hospital wards; hard on the outside, but this exterior protecting a more caring attitude.

The avoidance of caring by prison officers may also be legitimate. Having a personality disorder (as most prisoners do) means that one's psychopathology is expressed in relationships. Whereas psychotic patients' psychopathology is manifested in their own mind in the form of delusions and hallucinations and neurotic or depressed patients suffer with their compulsions, or anxiety, or whatever it is, this is not the case with the personality disordered. Here, the psychopathology is actually expressed in the relationships that the person has, in the space or area of intimacy that opens up between two people who get to know each other. Usually, this area of intimacy, once established, is used for a psychological assault. This hurts, and it will be the daily experience of prison officers who work day in, day out with society's most disturbed personalities. After several such assaults, they will learn to hide any caring attitude they might have; indeed, the trauma may be so difficult to process that they will simply become phobic of the idea of engaging in a caring way with inmates.

The therapist in a prison becomes a focus for this anxiety about caring. Almost imperceptibly, it becomes clear that as a civilian with a task to care for prisoners, one is seen as a bit of a wimp, a bit soft. However legitimate one believes one's work to be, it somehow starts to seem worse than irrelevant, an indulgent waste of time. Therapy is antithetical to the required masculine ethos in the setting; therapy is for weaklings and by weaklings, and the attack is accelerated because it threatens the pre-genital macho compromise. Therapy in a prison setting is difficult to do.

The theme of concretization

Grendon Prison is an off-the-peg 1960s prison building, which from the outside is a big concrete wall. This wall in the Buckinghamshire countryside is about as far from a Viennese suburb as the Grendon inmates are from the middle-class neurotic patients that Freud first tried to treat with his developing psychoanalytic technique. Yet the therapeutic community treatment in Grendon is simply an application of psychoanalysis on an industrial scale. But this observation is not a comment on their different social class or other demographic characteristics; it is a comment on concreteness. Freud shocked turn-of-the-century Europe by suggesting that civilized people might have violent thoughts and unconscious ideas, that they might have murderous fantasies towards their nearest and dearest, that they might covet others' possessions, or that they might have incestuous or other grotesque sexual thoughts. The real difference between Grendon men and their middle-class Viennese psychoanalytic predecessors is that Grendon men haven't just thought these things—they've done them. Violence, killing, sexual offences, or whatever has not just been a fantasy or a bad dream: it has actually happened in concrete reality. Prison is very concrete. The containment is concrete; the enforcement of rules is concrete; the protest is concrete; and the crimes that people are incarcerated for are concrete enactments of common fantasies. The prison environment and its inhabitants are all imbued with a concrete air that is not conducive to a therapeutic process.

Aspects of prisoners' development have been concretized. Many of these men have not had the benefit of an oedipal phase carried out with loving and containing adults, but have had fathers or stepfathers who have all but killed them. Other developmental battles have been enacted in concrete reality rather than in a symbolic realm of ideas and fantasies. As a result, they cannot be contained within the ideational constraints of accepted behaviour—society's shared structure of what is right and wrong which we carry around in our minds. They have to have their boundaries enforced by the concrete arm of the law, by an external real force that constrains them. Having transgressed, they are literally concretely contained. They are serving sentences in concrete boxes specially strengthened to prevent escape, within high concrete walls that serve actually to separate them from the rest of society.

The mothering or caring of the prison is concretized. One surprising thing about Grendon inmates is how many of them have spent most of their adult lives in prison. Far from being the abusive thing that damages them further, prison has been their life-saver. In between dives into drug-related self-damage and near death, they receive a five- or ten-year sentence during which they are well fed, body-build in the gym, and receive overdue medical care. Prison for them is a maternal figure that cares for and looks after them, that feeds and clothes them and keeps them warm. But this mother is not an internal mental representation of a good-enough object that watches over them. This mother engulfs them in a concrete cell–womb within a concrete wall–body from which they cannot get away. This mother doesn't threaten to engulf them—it has engulfed them, and they cannot get out until the end of their sentence.

In a prison, the psychological process of projection becomes a separate wing, where the "rule 43" prisoners are placed, those sex offenders and others who need to be separated for their own safety. Inmates refer to "doing the numbers". Prisoners disavow their own evilness and project it onto those who have committed particular crimes, particularly sex crimes, or crimes of violence against women or children. This projective mechanism begins as a psychological process, but becomes concrete as people are assaulted and beaten because of the projections they have been allocated. This tendency can also be seen in Grendon where inmates describe psychic processes in concrete terms. For example, an inmate who has been affected or struck by a particular interpretation has had his "head battered". Projective identification is recognized in groups and referred to as "renting a room in someone else's head".

Therapy can be conceived of as a endeavour to reduce the need for concrete enactments of psychic conflicts. If clients can conceptualize and work through their murderousness toward their stepfather with an arts therapist or a psychological therapist, then the next father figure they meet might be a little safer; but it is important to realize that this endeavour fights against a tide of concretization and enactment that can seem overwhelming.

The staff trauma theme

In Gender and Players' authoritative account *Grendon: A Study of a Therapeutic Prison* (1995), they comment on the issue of the trauma of working with people who have committed crimes that one might find personally disturbing. They comment that their worry was unfounded: that after just a few days they were discussing the most horrendous crimes that inmates had committed in a straightforward and unemotional way. This account raises a fascinating conundrum, and a major difference in the task of the prison officer, or custodian, and the therapist. For the officer who has to work day in, day out with the inmate, who has to engage with him or her to facilitate everyday life on the prison wing, who has to manage aggression and resentment to prevent a riot, this sort of denial is entirely adaptive. Prison officers describe a process of separating the inmate from the crime; they can maintain respect and affection for the prisoner by splitting off and hating the crime as something separate.

The usefulness of these strategies can be argued from a variety of positions: that it would be counterproductive to keep hitting inmates over the head with how evil they have been; that everyday working relations require a modicum of mutual positive regard that might be impossible with an emotional engagement with the facts of the index offence; and, thirdly, for personal protection.

Prisons, especially "training prisons", where longer-term prisoners go, have concentrated populations of people who could give a shocking and disturbing story. Police detectives might make a whole career on the back of the solution of one particularly gruesome crime, and then be haunted by it for life. The average prison officer looks after twenty or thirty such cases each shift. If an officer spent his or her time contemplating a victim's last moments, or the state of mind of the perpetrator immediately preceding or after the event, or the suffering of the victim's family, he or she would be unable to carry on the work. Multiply this by twenty or thirty per shift, and he would definitely be unable to carry on the work. One might speculate whether Gender and Players had to swing into denial of the meaning and implications of inmate's crimes to be able to carry on their study. The situation is different for the prison psychotherapist.

The task of the therapist is to work with that discomfort, to be mindful of and work with the horror of the meaning of the crime. The task is also to explore the meaning of the crime; to explore its antecedents and immediate precursors; and to explore the attitude of the perpetrator to the victim in his or her terror, and to the suffering of the family bereaved by a violent crime. The exploration of the state of mind of the perpetrator in the moments leading up to the crime is crucial—understanding what happened, how the act was triggered, how the more normal prohibitions were overridden, and so on.

Prisons are difficult places for therapists, therefore, because their task requires them to relinquish the defences that make working in prison survivable for the majority of staff. However, I doubt the effectiveness of these defences. On one occasion shortly after arriving at Grendon, I was complaining about the number of keys that I always fumble with. "Working in a prison makes you much more aware of locks and bolts. I never locked anything in the house till I started", said an officer at the prison gate. I was struck by how, since working in the prison, I had become more vigilant about locking doors. On reflection I realized that I was more vigilant about other aspects of house security. I remembered that I had been thinking (apparently unrelatedly) about speaking to the children about strangers, and to my partner about security, rape alarms, and so on. There was obviously a link here which was confirmed by the fact that the security lapses in my own lifestyle which I had become aware of were linked to the crimes of residents that I had interviewed: several housebreakers, a rapist, and an offender against children.

Linked to this "symptom" of increasing security was another, more pervasive and pernicious reaction, which until the link was made had not made sense. It was like a pilot coming into land realizing that the undercarriage was suddenly malfunctioning—a sense of certainties being taken away, things that are vital and relied upon, things that are usually taken for granted. In my case, these things were a sense of security in my home and a confidence in the safety of my partner and children. As someone with an interest in severe personality disorders, and a doctor, as a rule I do not take personal safety and security as givens; however, there is a difference between being aware of the possibility of disturbing a burglar in your own house and spending time with someone who has killed a householder in such circumstances. This work adds a dimension of reality to these nightmares. Nightmares (and films about bad people) are fundamentally reassuring. The nightmare is a creation of one's own mind and therefore represents some sort of mastery over the fear. Films usually end with the rosy glow of the bad guy getting his just desserts, representing the film-maker's fantasy of mastery over the fear. In real life, no one has mastery, least of all the perpetrator in the psychotherapy session. The reaction of Gender and Players of relative indifference to the residents' crimes is the prevailing ethos in prison settings, and the forgoing comments might be criticized for being prosaic or over-dramatic. This may or may not be so. This is how it seems to a therapist newly in prison work, and from this position, if it seems any different with the passage of time, it's time to go.

My hypothesis is that prison staff use a variety of defensive mechanisms to keep at bay the meaning of the crimes that their inmates have committed, but that these defences are probably only partially effective. Prison staff work in an environment in which their sense of personal safety and security is undermined, which will be a chronic traumatic strain. For the prison therapist this will be relevant for two reasons. First, there will be a resistance by prison staff to contemplating the possibility that residents' index crimes have meaning and that the prisoner and the crime cannot be comfortably separated. So there will be an endemic resistance to therapy per se. Second, as is more common with therapy provided in institutional settings, the prison staff will envy the fact that prisoners are being provided with the sort of help that, at some unconscious level, they will be aware that they need themselves.

The theme of the client group

In looking at the client group as a whole and trying to describe how they differ from patients in private or NHS practice, one runs the risk of generalizing in a negative way. The practice of projecting things into one's client group will be familiar to all therapists, but this process can be more problematic when, by and large, the projections that the client group invite are pretty negative, as is the case with the longer-stay prison population. Nevertheless, it cannot be avoided that if personality-disordered people cause "themselves or society to suffer", then this prison group has a preponderance of severely personality-disordered people.

There is a sceptical view of the diagnosis of "borderline personality disorder" by psychoanalytic therapists, which is that the term is synonymous with "my worst patient". Surely someone who has sufficient ego strength to get into analytic therapy and is able to pay and sustain the work must be healthier or more together than someone who ends up in psychiatric hospital and sees an analytic therapist on the NHS. By the same token, someone who ends up in prison is the most disturbed. The ego functioning, the reality orientation, of such people has been insufficient to enable them to tolerate the frustration of their immediate desires, their aggression has not been constrained by the ego's diplomacy, and they have ended up on a long sentence. Arguably, in any society the largest provider of services for the severe personality disordered is the prison service.

Does this mean that the prison population is the same as a therapy population in the NHS or private practice, only more disturbed and fragmented? Alternatively, are there broad differences between the groups of patients? Have private practice patients found a defensive niche of carers or relatives that can pay for therapy, but are otherwise fragmented? Does it mean that NHS patients will be those whose aggression is directed inwards as suicidality or self-harm, or those who flip into psychosis? Using such a common-sense approach, in prison one might expect a preponderance of those whose difficulties are expressed by actual violence, or those who use substances and end up stealing or robbing to fund this. To some extent this is true. The aggression on prison landings is palpable; it is like wallpaper—ubiquitous and impossible to avoid. It gets everywhere, from snide nicknames to accurate and hostile teasing, from the psychological assault of complaints and litigation to the frank assault using fists and a variety of other makeshift or smuggled weapons.

The Prisons Act from the nineteenth century stipulates that, in addition to a jailer, a prison must have a doctor and a chaplain. In the dialectic of prison management, the care/control argument often comes to a head over medical issues: whether a prisoner is "fit" to be moved, or whatever. So the role of the prison doctor is, to some extent, that of the generic carer. Men in prison visit the doctor vastly more frequently than men of the same age group in the community, implying that medical care somehow substitutes for the deprivation that is most of prison life. However, the difference between being a GP in the NHS and doing the same work in the prison service revolves around this issue of aggression. In prison, everything is currency. If an inmate can obtain a prescription for a sleeping tablet, he might sell it to the highest bidder; if an inmate can get a prescription for shampoo, this also has its price. Woe betide the brave medic who tries to make a stand against this manipulation: complaints and litigation will rain down. The doctor–patient relationship ceases to be an interaction where a benign paternalism holds sway; instead, an aggressive and abusive exchange takes place, probably transferential, to previous father figures. An attempt is made to destroy entirely the doctor's professionalism. Prison doctors anecdotally report patients who have presented in the hope that things will be mismanaged so they will be able to sue and make some money from the settlement.

Another manifestation of this aggression is when it simply boils out in a torrent of screaming violence. There is a very clear difference between someone who is "fighting mad" and someone more conventionally psychotic, however disturbed they are. The loudest, most persistent, most forceful, most destructive, and so on is the person who is "fighting mad": they can go on for hours or days in an intense communication with whoever has to listen to them banging the door and screaming. The volume of rage that people can possess is astounding, and it is possessed by most people who end up in prison for long periods. Indeed, many index and previous offences will have been committed while in such a state.

Another main differentiating feature of prisoners as a group concerns the issue of lying. This is an issue that, when working with this group of people for the first time, is both bewildering and shocking, and then obvious and second nature. In her paper on psychoanalysing a liar, O'Shaughnessy (1990) describes starting an analysis with access to the usual sort of information reported by the patient, and then finding out bit by bit that it was all false. The effect of this attack on the beliefs of the analyst was profound and disturbing, and the question posed was whether analytic therapy was possible given the requirement to be truthful with the thoughts and fantasies that cross the patient's mind. On the other hand, the lies might prove as fertile material for analysis as the dreams or accounts of reality that might be brought. In addition, the fact of the lying, the reasons for, and so on become a central analytic focus.

In a prison setting, the situation is reversed. One of the few things that one can be absolutely sure about in what inmates say is that a good proportion is untruthful. Untruthfulness is a sort of language from which the truth has to be decoded. An alternative way of looking at it is that the truth is defined by a particular moment or by a particular contact. Inmates will tell well-meaning therapists what is right for that interaction, what seems right, what they want to hear. Truth in the interaction is more like truth in a theatre. Watching *Macbeth*, one is not transported to Cawdor Castle in Scotland, the players do not become the people they portray. And yet, in another way, one is transported and the players do become the protagonists. The cast are not engaged in a deception: there is a mutually agreed suspension of truth for the duration of the play, and fantasy becomes reality. Truth and falsity in a prison setting is similar to this: it has a dramatic quality.

Negotiating and working with prisoners requires a third eye, something similar to Freud's "evenly suspended attention" of the psychoanalyst. And an awareness is required that one will frequently get it wrong. For the therapist, this is quite important because, working with a patient for a period, one builds up a complex picture that becomes personally legitimate, a picture and opinions that one feels confident about. It seems that in a prison setting, these therapeutic opinions have to be even more qualified than they do usually. Often, crimes are committed by only part of a fragmented personality, and there is a risk that in the same way a therapy that is meaningful for the therapist is being conducted with one of the prisoner's false selves. In the Grendon communities, being able to be truthful is a central element in the therapeutic process. An inability to be truthful is conceived of as starting during an abusive childhood. The abuser insists on the truth being suppressed on pain of violence, humiliation, or even death. This habitual secrecy protects the abusive experiences from disclosure and ends up being used as a principle defensive strategy in the protection of the self from any sort of intimacy.

The prison population is different in a number of ways from the usual people who present for psychotherapy. In addition to having particular and severe personality difficulties often manifested by violent acting out, they have been conditioned into blurring the boundaries of truth and falsity. Both of these factors present considerable technical problems for the therapeutic process which have to be borne in mind in the assessment of patients' suitability for therapy and in the process of treatment.

The Grendon therapy/security dialectic

What do you do in a psychotherapy session where an angry patient arrives with a loaded gun? Do you carry on the session as normal, trying to understand what it means, what has prompted it? Or do you refuse to see him and call the police? Calling the police is an enactment of the anxiety generated; doing therapy with an angry patient carrying a gun is a bit mad. In this apocryphal analyst's dilemma lies the kernel of the therapy/security dialectic. How long can you carry on doing therapy safely? In Grendon, the debate between security and therapy is one of crucial but creative conflict. The issue can be seen in three different ways. First, that the promotion of security directly conflicts with therapy; second, that security actually facilitates therapy; and third, that in fact therapy provides security.

Security and therapy in conflict

The conflict between security and therapy is easy to see. Group therapy requires that Grendon residents be able to sit in groups (therapy) rather than be locked in their cells (security). If a staff member develops a suspicion that an inmate is intimidating others, the member can either bring this up in a community meeting and try to get the issue into the open (therapy) or brief prison intelligence (security). If it is confirmed that a resident has made a weapon, the resident can be either challenged about it to explore the reasons and meaning of this (therapy) or "lifted" and put in a segregation unit (security). In each of these cases, the "solution" to the problems from a security and a therapy perspective are polar opposites. Furthermore, the security solution is actually destructive of the attempt to deal with the problem therapeutically. Confining people to their cells destroys the possibility of a therapy group; secretive amassing of suspicion prevents dialogue and therapeutic interaction; putting someone in the segregation unit out of the community destroys that person's therapy.

In response to a threat, the security side advocate action. The discussion is pushed towards closure, pushed towards a plan that can be executed, done and finished—the man is moved. Therapy advocates the opposite: action is viewed as an enactment of the anxiety until proven otherwise. The impetus is towards opening up discussion in an attempt to develop an understanding of the dynamics, rather than pushing towards closure and an action plan. For therapy, the important thing is to delay, to contain, and to think. Perhaps the resident's therapeutic struggle has become too great and the weapon conveniently forces removal, saving him from having to work the issue through. Any possible understanding such as this is lost as he is bundled out.

So, therapy is about voluntarily exploring "meanings" and "reasons" for things, to establish greater freedom. Prison is about the compulsory restriction of this exploration and the curtailment of freedom for those "committed by the courts". Therapy "thinks" and tries to do as little as possible. Prison "does" and tries to think as little as possible. The two approaches to the drugs issue illustrate this. The push from the security side is to "do" things—a new policy, more tests, more searches, better intelligence, more dogs, a new unit. The push from therapy is to "think"—why the panic, why the increase, why the policy, why the proposals, why the perception of a problem in the first place? Security drives therapy mad because the frenetic activity of doing things is like a dog chasing its tail and puts therapy off thinking and coming up with hypotheses. Therapy drives security mad because therapists never actually do anything. In a burning building they would comment on the pattern of the flames instead of getting water.

Part of the value of Grendon is that it shows that an establishment can balance the two so that a genuinely therapeutic milieu is possible; however, that does not mean that the different angles disappear. They still present potent alternatives about how to proceed with a given problem. The task that faces the Grendon community staff team is to debate the various alternatives and to come up with a decision that balances the competing requirements of therapy and safety. This is achieved by virtue of the multidisciplinary staff team. Uniformed officers, professionals in risk assessment, riot management, hostage negotiation, and so on sit with the therapist, the psychologist, and the probation officer who comprise the staff team to discuss the problem and how it should be managed. With a unity of aim, which is to maintain the therapeutic work of the community, they hammer out a compromise that maintains the safety and functioning of the therapeutic community while going as far as possible to maintain the therapeutic input to the index inmate.

Security facilitating therapy

Security provides containment. I have argued that the walls of the prison, the bolts, the bars, and the physical security, represent a concrete containment. Grendon is a prison first, and a therapeutic community second. It is a prison in which there is a therapeutic community regime, and in the therapeutic team the majority of the therapeutic staff—the "front-line" workers—are prison officers. Having prison officers as the primary deliverers of therapy is very different from having a nurse or care worker as the primary carer. In a prison, a prison officer is a constable of the law. In a prison, disobeying the direct order of a prison officer is an offence. In a prison, the officer maintains good order and discipline with a watertight legal framework of authority. If a prisoner misbehaves, or is even verbally abusive, the officer reports this and an adjudication is held, like a mini-court process in which the prison governor is the judge. Punishments from this mini-court can be quite significant, with prisoners receiving extra days or weeks added on to their prison sentence. This process is rigorously monitored and at times legally contested by prisoners' representatives, but nevertheless the prison officer has potent and clear authority to maintain "good order and discipline".

My contention is that this absolute authority of the prison officer is essential to the therapy in Grendon. The client group at Grendon contains some of the most disturbed and dangerous people in the country, with high scores on the indices of personality disorder and high psychopathy scores. In the communities, the staff members open themselves up to therapeutic engagement with this client group, and in the process they are traumatized and tested. What makes it possible for them to be able to take this risk is the security of the containment that surrounds the work: not only are there alarm buttons in every room, but also the staff have "control and restraint" training and riot training; they also have (when the chips are down) the absolute authority conferred by their officer status.

Nevertheless, there is a paradox here. A psychodynamic interpretation can only ever be a hypothesis that the patient is free to accept or reject. Suppose that an officer interprets to a prisoner that the officer is hated by the inmate because he represents the authority of the prisoner's hated and abusive father. Technically, the officer can order the inmate to accept this interpretation, and report him to the Governor if he refuses. It seems astonishing that such a situation can support a therapeutic process, but two crucial factors enable this to happen. The first is careful guidance and supervision from the psychodynamically orientated members of the team. This enables the officers to develop their native empathetic and therapeutic skills; indeed, many become effective community workers and skilled group facilitators. The second factor is a line management supportive of the therapeutic aims. The quasi-militaristic nature of the prison service authority structure means that the Governor's orders are to be obeyed. If the governor's order to the officers is to do therapy and to follow the lead set out by the community psychotherapist, then this is what they will do to the best of their ability. After a while, the officers' therapeutic skill and their recognition of the legitimacy and usefulness of the approach becomes autonomous, and the therapeutic ideology is established.

Therapy is security

The third perspective of the therapy/security dialectic is simply that therapy is security. Therapy dismantles some of the psychopathology that makes people a security risk, and it does this in three distinct but related ways. First, specifically in relation to Grendon and other therapeutic community settings, prison residents back a sense of belonging. Being in a community removes the Durkheimian prison anomie that grants the prisoner destructive licence. Instead, he is a member of a respected group of peers who uphold a set of community-derived or community-endorsed mores. Partly from the inherited culture and partly by trial and error, he comes to realize the personal benefits that accrue from "good order and discipline", and as a result his risk potential diminishes.

The second factor comes from the recognition of the humanness of the prison situation. The frosty and hostile interaction between Officer John (Smith) and E205 Eddie (Jones) during a cell search operation becomes a piece of work that John and Eddie both have to get done; both would prefer to be playing pool, and both would prefer to be at home with their kids. For Grendon residents, the staff become important people with a professional task whom they want to support, rather than the "screws" they proclaim they want to kill.

Third, and perhaps most importantly, as the therapy begins to permeate the residents' understanding of their crime and themselves, they begin to accept the legitimacy of their incarceration. This enables them to recognize and, most importantly, accept their role as prisoners.

These changes—the establishing of the ability to engage in and sustain intimacy and trust—are the basic building blocks of security. These enable the resident to feel secure in a containing and caring environment perhaps for the first time in their lives.

If they feel more secure in themselves, the compulsion to be threatening and to project their insecurity out onto the observer diminishes, along with some of their violence.

Conclusions

In this chapter, the therapeutic communities in Grendon Prison have been briefly described and the nature of a prison environment has been looked at in terms of concretization, the client group, anxieties about caring, and the trauma on staff. I have suggested that therapy and security are, at the same time, in conflict, facilitative of each other, and even synonymous. Running through this account has been the theme of the paradox of therapy in a prison. In Grendon, this paradox focuses the ideological tensions between security and therapy. These tensions are a constant struggle, but a creative one that fires the quality of the work. However, in other prison settings, the therapy/ prison paradox can be experienced purely as an irritation which is all too easily removed.

The "therapies", with their poor record of empirical verification and their controversial metapsychology, are poorly suited to a prison environment, which values uncomplicated simplicity and clarity. Yet the prison client group, from deprived backgrounds and living in an environment of deprivation, are receptive to these therapeutic approaches. Therapy in this setting provides some sense of meaning for what has happened in their lives, some way of understanding it all, some way of beginning to knit together the people that they are. It is clear that the process of integration of these fragmented people in therapy will reduce their need to enact their psychic conflicts in offending behaviour. As a result, the importance of this work is underlined. Therapists in prison not only have the responsibility of trying to recover their patients, but must also keep in mind the possibility of there being future victims. As well as being very difficult, this work is crucially important.

REFERENCES

Bion, W. (1967). On arrogance. In: *Second Thoughts: Selected Papers on Psychoanalysis* (pp. 86–92). New York: Jason Aronson. [Reprinted London: Karnac Books, 1984.]

Cheifetz, L. G. (1984). Framework violations in psychotherapy with clinic patients. In: J. Runey (Ed.), *Listening and Interpreting: The Challenge of the Work of Robert Langs* (pp. 215–252). New York: Jason Aronson.

- Etchegoyen, R. H. (1991). *The Fundamentals of Psychoanalytic Technique*. London: Karnac Books. [Reprinted London: Karnac Books, 1999.]

Freud, S. (1916). Some character types met with in psychoanalytic work. Criminals from a sense of guilt. In: *Standard Edition, Vol. 14* (pp. 332–333). London: Hogarth Press, 1957.

Gallway, P. (1965). Prison structure and criminal aggression. *Sixth International Congress of Psychotherapy, London 1964: Selected Lectures*. New York: Karger.

Gender, E., & Players, E. (1995). *Grendon: A Study of a Therapeutic Prison*. Oxford: Clarendon Press.

Hinshelwood, R. (1993). Locked in a role: a psychotherapist within the social defence system of a prison. *Journal of Forensic Psychiatry, 4* (3): 427–440.

113

• Hinshelwood, R. (1996). Changing prisons, the unconscious dimension. In: C. Cordess & M. Cox (Eds.), *Crime, Psychodynamics and the Offender Patient* (pp. 464–474). London: Jessica Kingsley.

Hyatt Williams, A. (1998). *Cruelty, Violence and Murder: Understanding the Criminal Mind.* London: Karnac Books; Northvale, NJ: Jason Aronson.

Klein, M. (1934). On criminality. In: *Love, Guilt and Reparation and Other Works* (pp. 258–261). London: Hogarth Press & The Institute of Psychoanalysis, 1985. [Reprinted London: Karnac Books, 1992.]

Knowles, J. (1997). Women who murder their children. In: E. V. Welldon & C. Van Velsen (Eds.), *A Practical Guide to Forensic Psychotherapy* (pp. 84–87). London: Jessica Kingsley.

Langs, R. (1979). *The Therapeutic Environment.* New York: Jason Aronson.

Main, T. (1989). Some psychodynamics of large groups. In: *The Ailment and Other Psychoanalytic Essays* (pp. 100–122), edited by J. Johns. London: Free Association Books.

Menzies Lyth, I. (1959). The functioning of social systems as a defence against anxiety. In: I. Menzies Lyth (Ed.), *Containing Anxiety in Institutions* (pp. 43–83). London: Free Association Books.

O'Shaughnessy, E. (1990). Can a liar be psychoanalysed? *International Journal of Psychoanalysis, 71*: 187–195.

Rosenfeld, H. (1965). The psychopathology of drug addiction and alcoholism: a critical review of the literature. In: *Psychotic States: A Psychoanalytic Approach* (pp. 217–242). London: Hogarth Press. [Reprinted London: Karnac Books, 1985.]

Steiner, J. (1993). *Psychic Retreats.* London: Routledge.

Taylor, C. (1997). A case of murder. In: E. V. Welldon & C. Van Velsen (Eds.), *A Practical Guide to Forensic Psychotherapy* (pp. 103–110). London: Jessica Kingsley.

Welldon, E. V. (1988). *Mother, Madonnna, Whore: The Idealisation and Denigration of Motherhood.* London: Free Association Books. [Reprinted London: Karnac Books, 1998; New York: The Other Press, 1998.]

Williams Saunders, J. (in press). Living on the edge: reflections on the addictive and intoxicating nature of working in a women's prison. *Free Associations Journal.*

Winnicott, D. W. (1965). *The Maturational Processes and the Facilitating Environment.* London: Hogarth Press.

Zachary, A. (1997). Murderousness. In: E. V. Welldon & C. Van Velsen (Eds.), *A Practical Guide to Forensic Psychotherapy* (pp. 79–83). London: Jessica Kingsley.

INDEX